PUT YOUR
Stamp ON IT

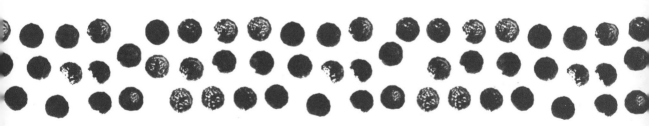

PUT YOUR *Stamp* ON IT

Meagan Lewis

20 ADORABLE PROJECTS

plus INSTRUCTIONS FOR HAND-CARVING BEAUTIFUL STAMPS

CHRONICLE BOOKS
SAN FRANCISCO

First published in the United States of America in 2013 by Chronicle Books LLC.

Copyright © 2013 by Quintet Publishing Ltd.

Library of Congress Cataloging-in-Publication Data available.

ISBN 978-1-4521-1571-9

Manufactured in China

Designer: Smith & Gilmour
Photographer: Marianne Paraskeva
Contributing Crafter: Gareth Butterworth
Art Director: Michael Charles
Project Editor: Ross Fulton
Editorial Director: Donna Gregory
Publisher: Mark Searle

10 9 8 7 6 5 4 3 2 1

Chronicle Books LLC
680 Second Street
San Francisco, California 94107
www.chroniclebooks.com

CONTENTS

INTRODUCTION

Stamping has been appreciated by both fine artists and crafters for a long time. Printmaking has been around for centuries. But what makes stamping currently so popular? As our world becomes increasingly dependent on technology and mass-produced items, handmade items gain even more value. How nice would it be to give a hand-stamped and personalized stationery set rather than a store-bought, generic box of cards? Or maybe you're getting married and can't find the right style of place cards and coasters. The solution can be as simple (and rewarding) as making your own.

You can make your own hand-carved rubber stamps, print your own gift wrap, and create a unique pattern to stamp on anything from a wooden picture frame to a cotton tote bag. These are just a few of the inspiring projects that will be outlined in this book.

I remember being about seven or eight years old and visiting a new mall with my mother. We went into a few shops but the one that stood out was a rubber stamp store. Yes, a whole store full of stamps! I admired all the stamps that filled the store walls from floor to ceiling. I wanted to take every stamp home with me. When I began to study printmaking some ten years later, I started to make my own stamps and used them to create handmade cards. It was so much fun not only to create the stamp but to come up with the design. The finished stamped piece—a card, a journal, or a gift tag—looked completely different than anything available in a store.

There are so many facets to printmaking, and each and every technique is truly exciting. I love the bold graphic shapes made from a screen print, and the delicate lines of an etching; but above all, my favorite is relief printing. Relief printing is essentially stamping. It's one of the simplest methods of printmaking and it requires a relatively small amount of materials and space. The word "relief" refers to the raised or relief parts of the block that get inked and that are then printed. In this book, I'll explore several different forms of relief printing through different projects.

The most recognizable type of stamp is the kind made of rubber and affixed to a wood block, but there are actually many kinds of "stamps." A stamp can be made from wood, linoleum, rubber, or a variety of alternative materials—in fact, you can make a stamp from just about anything. Use the projects and techniques shown in this book as inspiration to create your own stamps, and experiment with this versatile and exciting medium.

DRAWING INSPIRATION

Creating art is a two-part process—having an idea then bringing it to life. The idea is what makes the piece special and unique. We all have different ideas and styles and so we are all capable of producing art that is one of a kind.

In order to tap into our creative side we need to ask ourselves, "What do I like? Which colors do I like? What excites me?" The answers to these questions could be right in your home. You may have certain colors in your wardrobe, or patterns in some of your home furnishings, that you didn't realize were repeated throughout the house. Maybe you like bold colors and striking graphics, or perhaps you prefer a softer palette and simple shapes.

Consider getting a sketchbook and sketching ideas when they come to you. You can even cut out any images or colors that you like from magazines and glue them into your sketchbook. By observing and taking an inventory of the things you like, you may find yourself inspired to create a motif of a pattern that would be a great design for a stamp.

All of the projects featured in this book can be customized to your liking. I welcome you to change the colors, sizes, or layout of any of the designs. I hope that once you learn the basic steps to creating a stamp, you will try your hand at sketching some motifs of your own. You are only limited by your imagination!

MATERIALS AND TOOLS

There are many tools and materials available for creating stamps and printing. Many of these materials can be found at your local arts and craft stores, hardware stores, and online specialty stores. You may want to experiment with some tools or materials that I don't list in the book, and by all means, go ahead! Printmaking is an art of trial and error and experimentation. There are certainly some techniques, tricks, and a few rules to learn,

but as the artist you get to decide what kind of paper to print on, and what colors of ink to use. You may find an object around the house and think to yourself, "I wonder what would happen if I inked that up and printed with it?" You might discover a new technique or an interesting pattern by doing so. To get you started, I list the materials that you will find most helpful on the pages that follow.

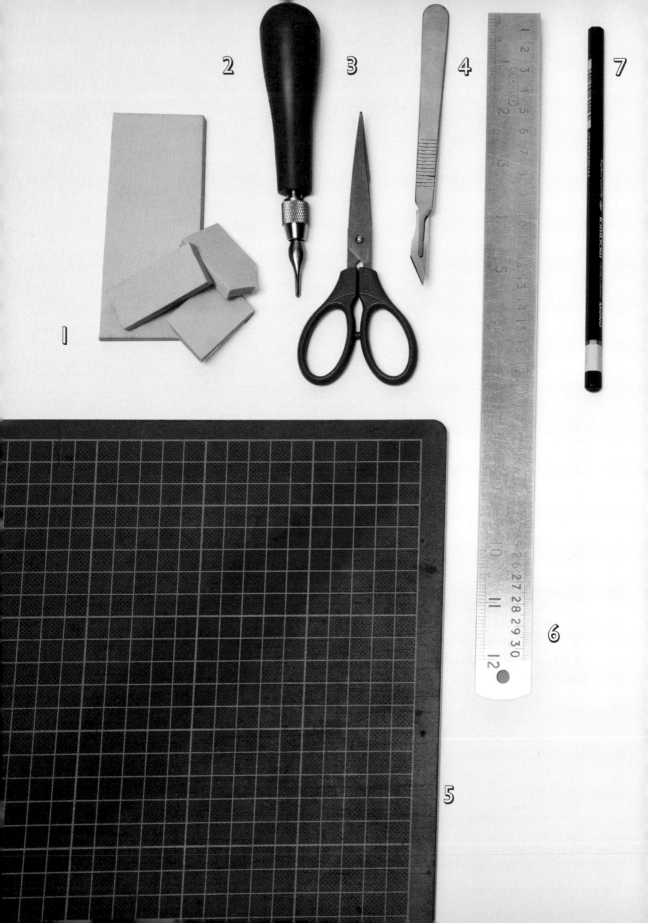

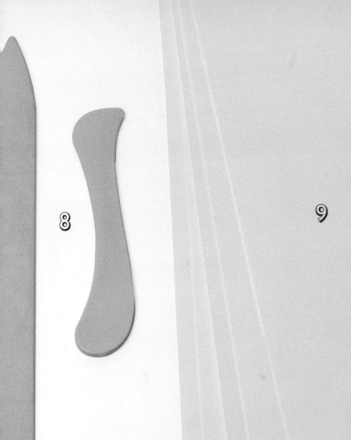

8

9

BASIC CARVING MATERIALS

These are the materials you will need to create a hand-carved
rubber stamp. Refer back to this list for many of the stamp projects
in this book. (See pages 12–13 for a more detailed description of
these items.)

1 Artist carving rubber
2 Linoleum cutting tool
3 Scissors
4 Craft knife
5 Cutting mat

6 Metal ruler
7 Graphite pencil (6B)
8 Bone folder
9 Paper

Artist Carving Rubber

As you start to gather your stamp-carving supplies, you may be delighted (or possibly overwhelmed) to see that there are many carving materials available. They range in color, texture, thickness, and density. Fortunately many of the materials come in precut sizes and are relatively inexpensive, so you can purchase a few different kinds and see what works best for you. For most of the projects in this book, a softer artist carving rubber is the best option. For most carving rubbers, both sides are the same and you may carve from either side. I like Speedball brand's Speedy-Carve. It's durable, easy to carve, easy to clean, and easy to print with by hand, whether it's mounted or unmounted.

Linoleum Cutting Tool

A linoleum (or lino) cutting handle and blade attachments can be found together in a set. You will likely get about five or six assorted blades in a set. The blades will vary from a thin V-shape blade (#1) excellent for carving the outline of a design and cutting fine detail, to a wide U-shape blade (#5) that will help you carve away larger areas. You may also get a flat blade (#6) for cutting and slicing. Do you need all of these? Well, perhaps not. Experiment with the blades and see what works best for you. I do all of my carvings with three blades: #1, #2, and #5. Because I use my tools so often I decided a while back to purchase three separate handles, one for each of the three blades I use. This way I don't have to change the blade every time I need to switch. When you do need to switch the blade from the

handle, twist the metal part at the end until the tip loosens and the blade can be carefully removed. You will see a slight opening where you can insert the new blade, then tighten the screw part to secure into place. Depending on how much you use your tools, you might not have to replace the blades very often. When carving becomes tougher than usual, or the blade no longer cuts a crisp edge, it's time to replace the blade.

Scissors

A good pair of scissors can go a long way. Look for a pair that is specifically for paper and has a nice comfortable handle.

Craft Knife and Cutting Mat

These two tools will come in handy for all sorts of things such as cutting rubber from a larger sheet. Choose a knife with a straight, replaceable blade. There are many cutting mats available. Look for a self-healing mat, 8 x 10 in/20 x 25 cm or larger, that has measurements printed on it.

Metal Ruler

While you can use a wooden or plastic ruler, a metal ruler will prevent you from accidentally slicing into it with your knife, and it won't chip or warp with time. The metal is also easy to clean if ink or graphite gets on it.

Graphite Pencil

There are many different kinds of artist pencils available. Graphite pencils, excellent for drawing and sketching, vary in hardness. Soft graphite pencils produce a bold dark line, and hard graphite will sharpen to a crisp point and produce a fine line. To get a stamp design transferred onto the carving rubber, you'll need a soft graphite pencil. A 6B graphite pencil works nicely. If you can't find a 6B, the graphite pencil scale below will help you to select something close.

Bone Folder

This tool is used for transferring a design to the rubber. It will also help you create a nice crease and fold with assorted papers. Made from bone or plastic, one edge has a point and the other a round or flat end. A Teflon material bone folder will be more expensive than a folder made of other materials, but Teflon is preferred because it will not mar or create an unwanted sheen on your paper.

Paper

The type of paper to use is likely going to be determined by the project you're working on. When testing prints (proofing), newsprint or copy paper will do the trick. For a nice print that you plan to frame, seek out a specialist printmaking paper such as Rives BFK. It's a cotton paper that is acid-free and has a soft feel that lends itself perfectly to printing with a variety of inks. If you're having a hard time selecting the right paper at a store, ask for help. A store associate should be familiar with the papers on hand and be able to help you find the right paper for your project. When stamping your own handmade cards or scrapbook embellishments, you'll find it easiest to use a pack of card stock or prepackaged blank cards and envelopes, all readily available in most craft stores.

Graphite Pencil Scale

light   dark

| F | H | 2H | 3H | 4H | 5H | 6H | 7H | 8H | 9H | H | HB | B | 2B | 3B | 4B | 5B | 6B | 7B | 8B | 9B |

good

OTHER MATERIALS AND TOOLS

These are a few of the most common materials and tools needed to complete many projects in this book. (See pages 16–18 for more a detailed description of these items.)

1 Ink pads
2 Block printing ink, water soluble
3 Paint (acrylic or specific type listed in projects)
4 Brayer and inking plate
5 Sponge daubers
6 Embossing heat gun
7 Eraser
8 Tape

You may also need:
Foam roller
Ink retarder and ink extender
Epoxy/glue
Adhesive mounting foam
Stamp blocks
Cloth towel
Stamp cleaner

4

5

6

7

8

Ink Pads

There are three basic kinds of ink pads: Chalk, dye, and pigment.

Chalk ink pads produce a chalky matte print. They come in a variety of colors from many different brands. The pastel colors available work nicely on darker papers.

Dye ink pads are probably the most common type of ink pads. The type of ink pads you see in an office supply store are dye-based, but I recommend seeking out those offered at your local craft store. You will find a large selection of colors from many brands. The dye ink pad will produce a crisp and relatively dark print. Both chalk and dye ink will dry quickly after printing.

Pigment ink dries more slowly then chalk- and dye-based inks. It is a rich, opaque, and vibrant ink that comes in a vast array of colors. Pigment ink prints very well with handmade stamps—the ink, similar to paint, sticks to the surface of the stamp and prints evenly. The slow drying time is ideal for embossing (see page 72). If you're not going to emboss but would like to use this ink, just make sure you let the print dry sufficiently or seal with a spray fixative.

Block Printing Ink

Block printing ink can be messy, but it's a lot of fun and the results can be quite delightful. I recommend going the route of block printing if you're (a) printing with a large stamp or (b) printing a lot at one time. You'll want to purchase the water-soluble type of ink, as it cleans up easily with warm water.

Paint

Paint can sometimes be the best option for your project. I'll explain which paints to use with the appropriate projects in the book, but if you're experimenting on your own, try acrylic paint. The main difference when printing with paint versus ink is that paint can be slippery and dries quickly. You might have to use less paint so that your stamp doesn't slide around when you print. Be sure to clean the paint off your stamp as soon as you're done printing. If paint dries on the stamp, it can be difficult to get off and will affect the quality of future prints.

Brayer and Inking Plate

A brayer is a rubber roller that will help you roll out block printing ink before applying it to the stamp. It's a very useful tool to help you control the amount of ink transferred onto the stamp. Be sure you have a flat surface to roll the ink out on before inking up your stamp—an old cookie sheet or an acrylic sheet from the hardware store both work well.

Sponge Daubers

These neat little tools, also known as sponge pouncers, are perfect for applying various paints to your stamp. The tool looks like a little stick with a small sponge at the end. They can be found in most arts and craft stores, likely in the stencil aisle. Unlike block printing ink (which utilizes a brayer), paint has a slippery consistency that needs to be applied differently. The sponge dauber allows you to pick up the right amount of paint and apply it evenly to the surface of the stamp. Wash the dauber with water when you're finished and it can be used over and over again.

Embossing Heat Gun

It's important to invest in a heat gun for embossing projects such as the one on page 70 and not use something else such as a hair dryer. The heat gun is specifically made for embossing—it heats up to a high heat and blows gently, which helps keep the embossing powder in place until it melts. Be careful with your heat gun! Follow all instructions and warnings on the package. Never put your hand in front of the tool and be sure to unplug it when finished.

Eraser

An eraser is useful for erasing registration marks or cleaning up a design before it is transferred to the rubber. Plastic or kneaded erasers are best; avoid pink erasers which can leave unwanted marks.

Tape

Double-stick tape is useful for mounting paper for card-making projects, or for temporarily affixing handmade stamps to a handle to make them easier to print with. Double-stick tape can be bought as a regular roll of tape, in a convenient dispenser, or as precut adhesive squares ("mounting squares").

Foam Roller

A foam roller is another great way to apply acrylic or fabric paint (not ink) to a stamp. The foam roller, because it is bigger than a sponge dauber, will allow you to apply paint to a larger stamp. Like the sponge daubers, a foam roller can be washed with warm water and used again.

Ink Retarder and Ink Extender

Add a small amount of **ink retarder** to your ink when you plan to make a lot of prints and you need to keep the ink fresh. It will help slow the drying time of your ink while you work. Only a little is needed relative to the ink, about 10 percent. A separate additive that you can mix with your ink is called **ink extender**. Adding in a bit of ink extender (at about 10:1 ratio to ink) will make your ink slightly transparent, ideal for printing overlapping colors and allowing the base color to faintly show through. This is especially helpful in reduction printing (see project 5 on page 54). Ink extender will also improve the consistency of ink that has become a little dry and sticky.

Epoxy/Glue

If you plan to mount any of your stamps, you'll need an adhesive to affix the stamp material to its mount. Though there are many ways to mount your stamp (see page 26), a strong glue is my go-to choice. Check out your local craft or hardware store for a good selection of adhesives that are suitable for use with the materials you are using. For example, if mounting a rubber stamp to a wood backing, then seek out an adhesive that works for both rubber and wood. I recommend an industrial-strength adhesive called "E-6000," because it is permanent and effective on a wide range of materials including rubber, wood, and plastic. Avoid using hot glue to mount your rubber stamps—the heat from the gun could melt your carving material.

Adhesive Mounting Foam

This foam, available online, comes in sheets that you can cut to the size of your stamp. Both sides of the sheet are coated with a strong adhesive that is exposed when you peel off the protective paper. It is very useful for mounting stamps to backing when you are in a hurry, as it adheres instantly.

Stamp Blocks

Also known as mounts, handles, or backings, stamp blocks can be the perfect finishing touch to your handmade stamps. Traditionally made of a smooth hardwood such as maple, stamp blocks can also be made of clear acrylic (plastic). Stamp mounts can be purchased at select arts and craft stores, or online. The acrylic type has become popular for use with clear photo-polymer stamps and cling stamps (rubber stamps that are mounted to a special "cling" foam). These kinds of stamps are typically sold as a sheet with assorted designs that get divided up and temporarily mounted to the acrylic block. The stamps cling to the acrylic block without any adhesive, and can easily be pulled off after being used. The benefit is that one block can be used with many stamps. This is ideal for crafters who have a large collection of stamps and need to conserve space—a few acrylic blocks of assorted sizes can be used with multiple stamps. When not in use, unmounted stamps can be stored in a special folder. These acrylic blocks are typically used for store-bought stamps, though they are also useful for handmade stamps. Rubber stamps will not cling to the acrylic but you can attach them with double-stick tape or glue. Besides wood and acrylic, there are alternative materials you can use to mount stamps. In this book, many projects call for good ol' plastic sheets from the hardware store. Basically the same thing as an acrylic block, an acrylic sheet (Plexiglass) can be purchased in larger sheets for bigger stamps. They also make great inking surfaces. See "To Mount or Not To Mount" (page 26) for more about mounting your stamps.

Cloth Towel

This is not really a tool but something worth having on hand. A cloth towel will be helpful when you need to wipe off inky fingers or clean your stamp. I recommend flour sack towels, which are soft, thin, and very absorbent. If you rinse the stamp in water, the towel can be used to pat the stamp dry. Paper towels are a poor substitute because they will leave lint on the stamp.

Stamp Cleaner

There are a variety of stamp cleaners available, many of which come as a spray that can be used with or without a cleaning pad. A cleaning pad can be helpful when cleaning ink out of a stamp's recessed areas; some pads have two sides—one should be saturated with stamp cleaner, and the other left dry. Rub the stamp onto the saturated side to remove the ink, and then blot or rub off the cleaner on the dry pad. If you have a cleaner but no pad, just spray some cleaner onto a paper towel and blot the ink off. Remember that stamp cleaner is only for removing the ink from ink pads—do not use stamp cleaner or pads to remove block printing ink or paint from your stamps (see opposite).

CLEANING AND CARING FOR YOUR STAMPS

Keeping your stamps clean is key to being able to enjoy them for many years. If ink is left to dry on your handmade stamp, it can fill in the recessed areas and affect the quality of future prints. It's also best to keep your stamps clean so that you don't end up with unwanted smudges of ink on other stamps, projects, or you!

The method for cleaning your stamp will depend on the materials you used to make it and the ink or paint that you used to print with. For unmounted, hand-carved stamps, simply wash them off with warm water and pat them dry with a soft cloth towel. For hand-carved stamps that you have mounted to a wood or acrylic backing, you'll want to avoid cleaning the stamp with water. Simply stamp off the excess ink onto scrap paper. Any remaining ink can be removed with a stamp cleaner or pad, a baby wipe, or by stamping on to a damp cloth (one you don't mind getting a little ink on).

Even after thoroughly cleaning your stamp, some staining may remain on the surface. Some inks will stain your stamp more than others. Rest assured that any staining is normal and will not damage your stamp. A lot of staining just means your stamp has been well loved and well used!

If you have used paint on your stamp, be sure to clean it off as soon as you're done printing. Paint dries very quickly and will be difficult if not impossible to remove if left on the stamp. The best way to clean paint off of your handmade stamp is to wash it in warm water and gently scrub the stamp with a soft toothbrush. Because water will be necessary to clean the stamp, I do not recommend mounting any stamp that you plan to use with paint.

Aside from keeping your handmade stamps clean, you'll want to store them in a place where they won't get scratched or damaged. Some carving rubbers are quite fragile and can scratch easily if they come into contact with any sharp or hard objects. Unfortunately the slightest unwanted chip in your stamp could ruin your design. I store my stamps individually in small gift boxes. Put a print of the stamp on top of the box so you know what's inside. Most rubber carving materials also need to be kept away from direct sunlight, which can harden the material and make it difficult to print with. Storing your stamps in a safe place will keep the rubber soft and like new.

HOW TO CARVE A STAMP

Each project in this book comes with a template that you can use to create a stamp by following the instructions below. You may also create your own designs and carve those into a stamp. The steps are the same for every stamp-carving project. I'll be sure to give you tips along the way, plus there are additional troubleshooting tips and techniques on pages 136–137.

There are many ways to get a design onto the carving rubber. I like to use photocopies because the paper is easy to draw on and you can protect your original design. Alternatively, you could use tracing paper; but because it's thinner, you'll want to make sure it doesn't wrinkle or tear when you burnish it onto the rubber.

1 Photocopy the design template; feel free to increase or decrease the size if you want.

2 Cut out the design and a piece of carving rubber to fit.

3 With your soft graphite pencil, trace the design of the template. Make sure not to smudge the graphite with your hand as you trace the design.

4 Carefully pick up the traced paper and place it face down on the rubber piece you just cut out. Holding the paper in place, gently burnish (rub) the back of the paper so that the pressure transfers the graphite to the carving rubber.

5 Lift the paper directly upward to remove. Your design should be transferred to the rubber and showing in reverse. For example, if you want to print words, you'd need to carve the words into the rubber so that they read backward.

6 Trim excess rubber about ¼ in/6 mm around design. You can bevel down the edges with your #5 tool to ensure they won't print.

7 Begin carving the stamp with the #1 blade (the finest cutter) to cut along the outside edges of the transferred design. You want to leave all of the areas on the stamp that have graphite (these are what will print) and carve away all of the surrounding areas (these will not print). Once you have carved the outlines, switch to a slightly larger blade (#2) and use it to widen the lines carved with the finer blade. Next, switch to an even larger blade (#5) to scoop away the remaining larger areas of rubber.

8 Repeat step 7 to refine the areas that were just carved. This will help deepen the recessed areas and sharpen the edges of the stamp.

9 Your stamp is now ready to print! Mount the stamp if you desire (see page 26 for mounting instructions) and print with your chosen method and inks.

Helpful Tips for Carving Your Stamp

◦ Always cut away from yourself and make sure you do not put your hand in front of the cutting tool.

◦ Hold the carving tool at about a 45-degree angle. Start cutting slowly and try to carve at an even depth.

◦ When carving a curve, move the rubber instead of the hand holding the blade. This will help you to create a smooth line.

◦ If you are right-handed, carve right to left. If you are left-handed, carve left to right. Never bend your wrist in an unnatural way to carve the stamp.

◦ Trim your stamp from the sheet of carving rubber, leaving a border of about ¼ in/6 mm around the design. Save any scrap pieces of rubber, as they can be used for smaller stamps or other projects (see project 18 on page 122).

THE RIGHT COMBINATION

To help you navigate the abundance of stamp-making materials available, here is a quick guide to help you determine which materials work best with various inks and paints. The opposite page gives some insights on printing surfaces and the effects you can achieve with different materials.

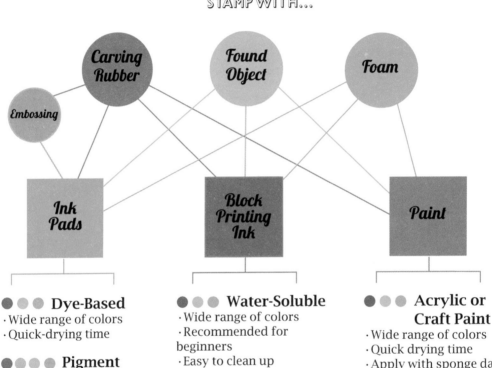

STAMP WITH...

Carving Rubber • *Found Object* • *Foam*

Embossing

Ink Pads • **Block Printing Ink** • **Paint**

● ● ● **Dye-Based**
· Wide range of colors
· Quick-drying time

● ● ● ● **Pigment**
· Rich, opaque colors
· Slower drying time

● ● ● **Chalk**
· Light, chalky colors
· Quick-drying time

● ● ● **Fabric**
· Limited colors
· May require heat-setting

● ● ● **Solvent**
· Limited colors
· Clean with solvent cleaner
· Ideal for alternative, non-porous surfaces

● ● ● **Water-Soluble**
· Wide range of colors
· Recommended for beginners
· Easy to clean up

● ● ● **Oil-Based**
· Limited colors
· Clean up with mineral spirits, turpentine or non-toxic alternatives made from soy or corn

● ● ● **Acrylic or Craft Paint**
· Wide range of colors
· Quick drying time
· Apply with sponge dauber or foam roller

● ● ● **Fabric Paint**
· Available in many colors and finishes (flat, gloss, metallic)
· May require heat-setting
· Apply to stamp with dauber or foam roller

Watercolor
· Unsuitable for stamping

Oil
· Unsuitable for stamping

STAMP ON...

Paper

■ Ink Pads
· Great for a variety of papers including cardstock, printmaking paper, and watercolor paper

■ Block Printing Ink
· Dries fairly quickly
· Great for framed prints and posters

■ Paint
· Works best with uncoated papers and dries quickly

Fabric

■ Ink Pads
· Use ink pads specifically for fabric
· May require heat-setting
· Pigment ink can be used but will not be permanent

■ Block Printing Ink
· Easy to work with
· May require heat-setting

■ Paint
· Easy to work with
· The addition of a fabric medium is recommended

Wood

■ Ink Pads
· Use ink pads specific for wood only
· Seal with varnish

■ Block Printing Ink
· Produces solid opaque print
· Can be sealed with varnisd

■ Paint
· Produces solid opaque print
· Stamp may slip when printing, so print carefully

Alternative Surfaces

■ Ink Pads
· Solvent ink pads may be used on a variety of surfaces such as glass, plastic, metal, and leather

■ Block Printing Ink
· Not ideal for surfaces other than paper, fabric, and wood

■ Paint
· Multipurpose paints can be used on a variety of surfaces. Follow manufacturer's instructions for clean up and care

CREATING VIBRANT COLORS

This mixing chart demonstrates how a variety of shades can be made by combining a few basic colors. Mixing your own colors is rewarding and fun, and a unique hand-mixed color will make your projects stand out beautifully.

Some colors are easier to create than others. For example, it may be difficult to make a vibrant magenta or turquoise by mixing only primary colors together, so you may opt to buy those instead. Black is not used in any of the examples shown here—black will certainly darken a color, but it will also make it dull. A dull or muted color may be exactly what you're looking for. However, if you are looking to darken the color yet retain its vibrancy, simply add the next darkest color on the color wheel. For example, add a little orange to yellow to create a warmer, darker yellow. Experiment, and have fun in the process.

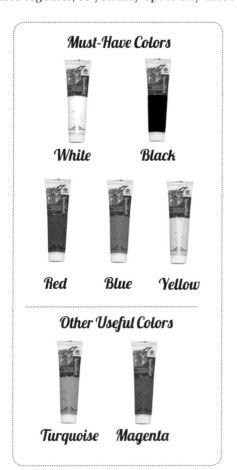

Must-Have Colors

White   Black

Red   Blue   Yellow

Other Useful Colors

Turquoise   Magenta

Extra Hints

What's the Right Amount of Ink?

To get the right amount of ink on the brayer, start with a little and add more as necessary. Not enough ink will produce a light or patchy print, while too much ink will produce a blurry, smeared print. Sometimes you can find the right amount by listening to the ink as it's rolled out. If it sounds loud and gloppy, you probably have too much ink—it should sound soft and quiet. Make test prints on scrap paper to help you find the right amount of ink.

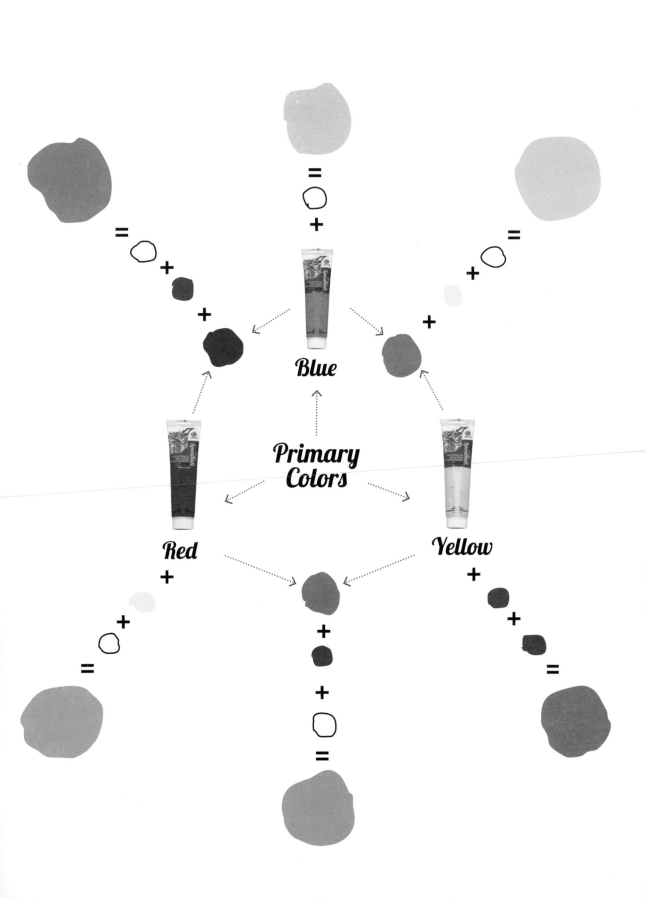

Blue

Primary
Colors

Red

Yellow

TO MOUNT OR NOT TO MOUNT

There is always plenty of room for trial and error in printmaking. Deciding to mount your stamp or leave it unmounted is completely up to you. There is a variety of mounting blocks available but you can also experiment with other materials—basically anything flat and sturdy that could be glued to the stamp.

There are benefits to both mounting a stamp and leaving it unmounted. A mount, wood or otherwise, can offer the printer ease of use. The mount will likely make the stamp easier to hold and lift away from the paper once printed. It can also help distribute pressure evenly when printing, which will help you achieve a clean, solid print. Additionally, a mount can be decorative and make your stamp look more like, well, a stamp! However, unmounted stamps can be ideal for projects where you need extra visibility to print the stamp, for example when you need to line up a series of stamps. The lack of a mount also makes the stamp easy to clean.

If you decide you would like to mount your stamp, here are some ways to do so. First you will need to decide what you would like to mount your stamp to—a piece of wood, a precut acrylic block, etc. To adhere the rubber to the backing, you can either use strong glue or epoxy, or you can use adhesive mounting foam. Glue will be easy to find at a craft or hardware store. You simply glue the rubber to the backing and wait until it dries before stamping. Alternatively, adhesive mounting foam will instantly adhere the stamp to the backing without any drying time. Another advantage to using foam is that the foam cushion helps absorb the pressure when you stamp, leaving you with a nice solid print.

UNMOUNTED VS. MOUNTED

Unmounted	Mounted
Easy to clean by rinsing directly in running water	Easy to hold
Easy to see where you're printing	Distributes pressure evenly
Suitable for small to medium stamps	Adds appeal and provides a finished look
Less expensive	Essential for larger stamps

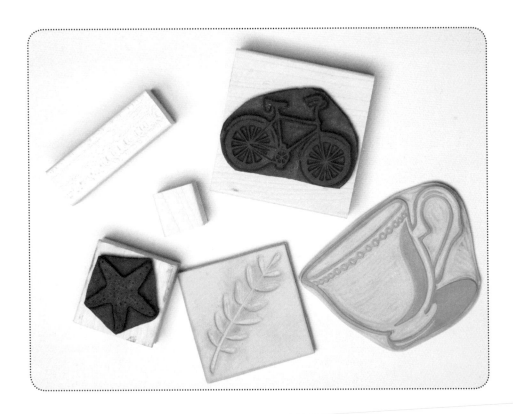

If you would like to temporarily mount your stamp to a backing, consider double-stick tape. This method is ideal for when you need to print individual stamps in a particular formation, but you don't want them mounted permanently. For example, in project 3 on page 44, I'll show you how you can use double-stick tape to position numbers in place, stamp, and then peel the stamps off when you're done. This is great when you need to print birthday numbers or wedding dates.

Most stamps that you see in stores show the image of the stamp printed on the wood handle, which helps you line up the design when printing. This print, called an index print, can be added to your own stamps. I like to stamp the wood handle with regular ink pads because I love to be able to use different colors. To do

this, print the stamp on the wood backing and let it dry. Then make the print permanent by brushing on wood sealer or a coat of clear acrylic varnish. Another option is to purchase special ink called indexing ink. It can be purchased in a bottle or in ink pads. The selection of colors is limited but the advantage is that because the ink is formulated for printing on wood (and in some cases on acrylic) handles, it does not need to be sealed. The third and final option I've found for indexing your stamp is really convenient if you're creating a large volume of stamps. Printable indexing sheets allow you to print your design right from your printer, cut it out, peel off a protective sheet, and stick it to your stamp mount. Printable index sheets for inkjet or laser printers are available online.

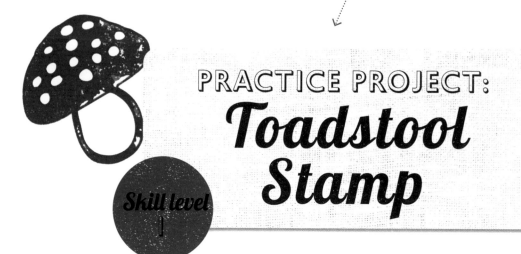

PRACTICE PROJECT:
Toadstool Stamp

Skill level 1

Materials

Basic carving materials (see page 10)

Utility knife (optional)

Fabric ink

Scrap paper

Template

Here's an easy project for practicing your carving skills. Decorate sweet gift tags, dish towels, and more!

1 Photocopy and print the toadstool template below at the size you would like to stamp it at. Cut out the design and a piece of rubber to fit. Then use a soft graphite pencil to trace over the printed areas of the stamp template on the paper, and place the paper face down on top of the piece of rubber you just cut out. Hold the paper in place, and use the bone folder to gently burnish (rub) the back of the paper so that the pressure transfers the graphite on to the carving rubber. Lift up the paper; your design should be transferred on to the rubber.

2 Start to carve the design, starting by using the finest blade (#1) to cut along the design's outside edges, leaving on all the areas on the stamp that have graphite on them, and carving out those areas left blank. Then switch to a larger blade (#2) to widen the lines.

3 Use a larger carving tool (#5) to remove the inside area of the toadstool's stalk, and all of the area outside of the templates outlines. You may want to go back over the areas which you just carved, deepening the recessed areas and smoothing the edges.

Stamp Tip

Don't forget your stamp will print the reverse of the picture you have carved. Think before you carve!

4 Wash your stamp with soap and water to remove any small pieces of cut rubber or pencil marks. Allow it to dry for a few minutes.

5 With your stamp facing up on a flat surface, wipe or dab the ink pad onto the surface of the stamp. Do a few test prints on a scrap piece of paper; you may see that you want to further refine your design. Now get stamping! It's worth noting that fabric paint or textilie screen printing ink may also be used on fabric. Turn to chapter 3 (page 90) for more information about printing on fabric.

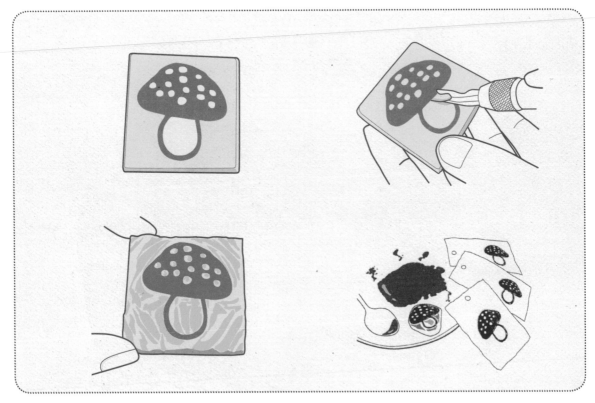

PROJECTS BY TECHNIQUE

While this book is organized according to each project's use ("Decorations," "Gifts," etc.), you may instead want to look up a project according to the particular technique or material used to make it. Here's a handy, at-a-glance guide to the stamping methods used throughout the book.

PRINTING FOAM

Skill level 3

Skill level 1

Skill level 2

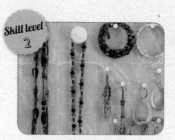

Project 9: Foam-Stamped Journals and Wrapped Pencils, page 76

Project 14: Printed Plaid Scarf, page 102

Project 19: Jewelry Organizer, page 126

RUBBER STAMP AND EMBOSSING POWDER

Skill level 1

Project 8: Embossed Monogram Stationery Set, page 70

FOUND OBJECT PRINTING

Skill level 2

Skill level 1

Project 12: Bubble-Wrap Tote Bag, page 92

Project 15: Pencil-Printed Bow Tie Hair Clip, page 106

Skill level 1

Skill level 2

Project 17: Thumbtacks and Magnets, page 118

Project 20: Dragonfly Shelf Liner, page 130

RUBBER

Skill level 1

Project 1: Coasters and Place Cards, page 34

Skill level 2

Project 2: Lined Envelopes, page 38

Skill level 2

Project 3: Number-Stamped Gift Wrap, page 44

Skill level 1

Project 4: Negative-Space Picture Frame, page 50

Skill level 3

Project 5: Reduction Printing, page 54

Skill level 2

Project 6: Coloring-In Stamps, page 60

Skill level 1

Project 7: Stamped Bookplates, page 66

Skill level 2

Project 10: Hand-Colored Floral Cards, page 82

Skill level 3

Project 11: Two-Colored Stamped Pillowcases, page 86

Skill level 2

Project 13: Kitchen Apron, page 96

Skill level 1

Project 16: Retro-Modern Storage Labels, page 114

Skill level 2

Project 18: Scrap Rubber-Decorated Storage Boxes, page 122

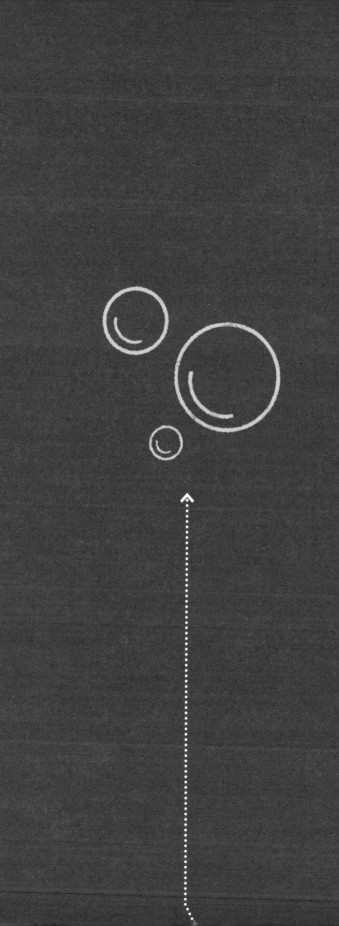

CHAPTER 1
Decorations

Stamping is an ideal method for decorating a wide range of items, from stationery to furniture. A stamp not only gives things a personal, handmade look that at the same time looks thoroughly professional, but it also allows you to build patterns and motifs that are visually striking and unique. By creatively using combinations of stamps, you can create an appropriate design for any occasion—from a classic and sophisticated wedding invitation to a fun and colorful picture frame. Experiment to find the most effective color scheme for your project, stamp it, then stand back and admire the results!

COASTERS AND
Place Cards

When entertaining, the dining table can be the focal point of your event. There are so many ways to bring a theme to life at the table. Easy-to-make bubble-design stamps create a fun and cheerful theme that can be repeated throughout your décor. Attractive coasters and place cards are a simple way to add elegance and charm. Consider stamping some other items such as favor bags or menu cards too. Any of these stamped items are sure to make your table shine. Cheers to that!

COASTERS AND PLACE CARDS

Skill level 1

Materials

Basic carving materials
(see page 10)

Water-soluble block printing ink

Brayer and inking plate

Blank paper coasters (made from
heavy card stock or chipboard)

Blank place cards or card stock

Putty knife (optional)

1 Photocopy the template and carve your stamps as instructed on page 20.

2 Lay your materials on a clean surface. Ensure that you have enough space for printing and a place to put the coasters and cards to dry.

3 Squeeze out a strip of block printing ink at the top of the inking plate. Roll the brayer into the ink and continue to roll it in a forward (not back and forth) motion until the ink is an even consistency.

4 Once you have the right ink consistency, place your stamps on a flat surface, carved-side up. Roll the ink onto the stamps and then pick one up and print. Repeat the inking of the brayer and stamps for each print. Try overlapping the bubbles and printing them in different colors. Let each color dry before printing the next.

5 Clean the brayer. Scrape up the remaining ink from the plate with a flat-edged tool such as a putty knife, then wipe with a wet paper towel or rinse with warm water.

Templates

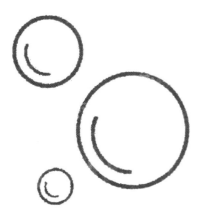

Extra
Hints

Decorate Your Table!

Select coordinating colors of linens, glassware, and flowers to make your handmade items pop. Other printed scraps can be made into gift tags or confetti.

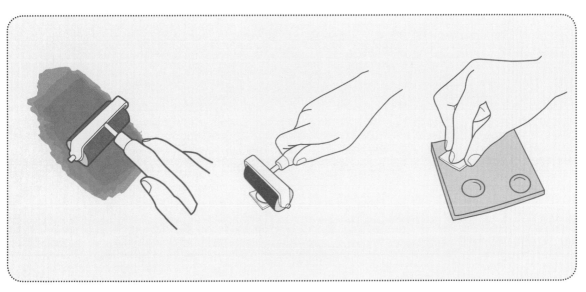

LINED
Envelopes

Lined envelopes are a simple way to add elegance to wedding invitations or any personal correspondence. Creating your own pattern on the lining paper gives an extra special touch. Any leftover stamped paper can be used to embellish the card or wrapped around a stack of cards to give as a gift. Experiment with the pattern stamp further by making your own gift wrap or scrapbook pages. The repeated pattern makes a striking design that is both modern and versatile.

LINED ENVELOPES

Skill level 2

Materials

Basic carving materials (see page 10)

Lining paper (lightweight paper such as handmade paper, rice paper, or text-weight stock)

Archival dye-based ink pad

Package of blank cards and envelopes

Card stock (one piece at least as tall and wide as your chosen envelopes with the flap open)

Double-stick tape

1 Photocopy the template on page 42, to a larger or smaller scale if you prefer, and carve your stamp as instructed on page 20.

2 Take your lining paper (any lightweight paper you have chosen) and visualize how you will stamp your repeated pattern. The stamp can be printed in a row or it could be printed in a checkerboard pattern with alternating colors.

3 Apply ink to your stamp and begin stamping on the paper. Repeat by stamping as straight and close to the last print as possible. Don't worry if you can't get each print to line up perfectly— any imperfections will add character. Set the stamped paper aside to let it dry.

4 While the stamped paper is drying, create a template for the envelope lining sheets. Have the piece of card stock, a ruler, and pencil to hand. You'll want to make sure that the height of the card stock is at least the height of the open envelope. Measure the width of the envelope. Make your template about ¼ in/6 mm narrower than the width of the envelope. Cut the card stock to its determined width.

5 Slide the cut card stock into an envelope and flip it over. With a pencil, lightly trace the edge of the flap of the envelope. Pull out the card stock and put it on a cutting mat. Take the ruler and slide it about ½ in/12 mm back from the line you have just made. Cut a parallel line approximately ½ in/12 mm in from the traced line so that when the lining is attached to the envelope, the envelope's adhesive strip is still exposed. Cut both angles. If the tip of the envelope is rounded, use a pair of scissors to round the corner. Slide your finished template back into the envelope to make sure that it fits.

6 To make the lining sheets, first determine the direction of the grain of the lining paper (see the "Extra Hints" box on page 42) and align your card stock template so that the envelope fold will be parallel with the grain. Using your template as a guide, cut out all the lining pieces.

7 Take a cut lining sheet and insert it into an envelope. Using a ruler and a bone folder, create a fold on the lining piece that matches the fold in the envelope (where the flap meets the pocket).

8 Fasten the lining to the inside of the envelope with a few pieces of double-stick tape. Close the envelope and run the bone folder along the edge to reinforce the fold and give it a crisp edge. Repeat for each envelope.

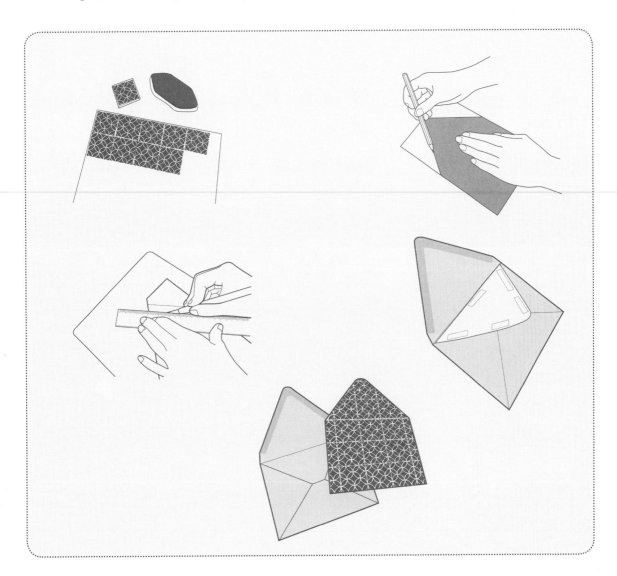

Project continues overleaf ⟶

Extra Hints

Establishing Your Paper's Grain

Before you cut the lining pieces out, you will want to establish your paper's "grain." All paper has a grain, and when creating a fold, you want to go *with* the grain, not against it or you won't get a crisp fold. To find the direction of the paper's grain, take the paper in the palms of your hands and gently attempt to fold it. Then turn the paper and repeat. Whichever way feels easier to bring together (has less resistance) is the direction of the grain.

Against the grain

Direction of the grain

Template

NUMBER-STAMPED
Gift Wrap

1
2
3
4
5
6
7

An essential part of every stamper's box of tricks, a set of number blocks will see you through a range of projects. Here you'll create your own gift wrap perfect for a birthday, anniversary, or wedding. If you're printing several numbers together, such as a date, the instructions tell you how to easily line the stamps up in order to print them together. Create stamped ribbon, gift tags, and cards to complete the coordinated look. This project could be adapted by using any font style or size you like, until you find that one perfect number stamp set.

NUMBER-STAMPED GIFT WRAP

Skill level
2

Materials

Basic carving materials (see page 10)

Wood or acrylic block (see "Extra Hints," opposite)

Blank wrapping paper, uncoated

Wide ribbon, satin or cotton

Dye-based ink pad

Double-stick tape

1 Photocopy the template and trace it with a soft graphite pencil. Transfer the design onto the carving rubber by using a bone folder to burnish the back of the paper, and then carve your stamp as instructed on page 20.

2 Lay the wrapping paper and ribbon out on a clean surface and decide how you would like to print your numbers. For example, you could print randomly, in a checkerboard pattern, or in a row.

3 Stamp the paper and ribbon as desired; be sure to re-ink the stamp before each print.

4 Let the paper and ribbon dry completely before wrapping gifts! Use double-stick tape to secure paper into place so that no tape will show and detract from your handmade gift wrap.

Templates

Number Font: Georgia (regular)

0   1   2   3

4   5   6   7

8   9   10

Printing with Multiple Numbers at One Time

Extra Hints

If you'd like to print a birthday or wedding date, you'll need a quick way to print the numbers together without having to worry about lining each number up to the next during the stamping process. To do this, take a wood or acrylic block long enough to fit your numbers in a line and double-stick tape the number stamps into place. Remember your numbers will print in reverse, so be sure to stick the numbers onto the block backward. The double-stick tape will secure the numbers to the block until you're ready to take them off.

Project continues overleaf ⟶

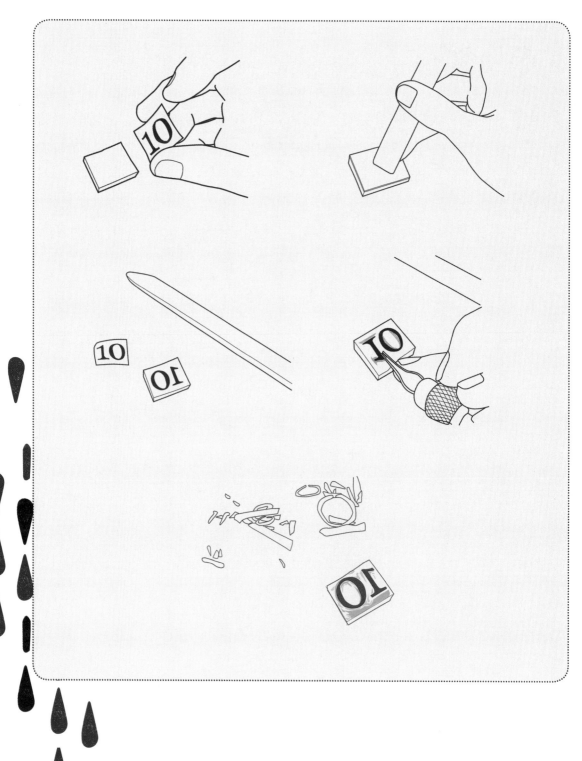

NEGATIVE-SPACE
Picture Frame

Negative-space stamps are an easy and effective way to show off intricate designs. The colors in this fun picture frame project can be customized to match your décor. Instead of stamping the design itself, you will carve the fern design away. The result is a lovely silhouette of the design that lets the base color of the frame show through.

You could also carve a letter, a word, or the profile of a loved one. The end result will surely impress—and did I mention that it's easy?

NEGATIVE-SPACE PICTURE FRAME

Skill level
1

Materials

Basic carving materials (see page 10)

Unfinished wood frame, 9 x 9 in/23 x 23 cm

Fine-grain sandpaper

Cloth

Paintbrush

Craft paint, a base color plus 1 color for stamping

Paper plate

Sponge dauber

Acrylic sealer clear coat

1 Photocopy the template and carve your stamp as instructed on page 20. However, once your design is burnished onto the stamp, instead of carving around the design, carve the non-penciled areas away. You will be carving the design away and leaving the background. If you have a different size frame than the one used to illustrate this project, scale the template up or down to fit.

2 Lightly sand the edges and surface of the frame with sandpaper. Remove any excess dust from the frame with a dry cloth. With a paintbrush, paint the base color onto the frame. Two coats should be sufficient. Set frame aside to dry completely.

3 Pour a small amount of the other color of paint onto a paper plate and sponge a bit onto your stamp using a dauber. Start by sponging a little bit of paint onto the stamp and add more as needed. Too much paint will fill in the recessed areas of the stamp and produce a blurry print.

4 Once your stamp is sufficiently coated with paint, pick it up and print onto your frame. Be careful not to let the stamp slide. Complete all of the stamping, re-inking the stamp between each print. Wash and dry the stamp, and set the frame aside to dry.

5 Once all the paint is completely dry, apply a clear coat of acrylic sealer to the frame, which will give it a nice smooth and durable surface.

6 When the acrylic finish is dry, insert your favorite picture, and admire the new piece of art that you have created!

Template

REDUCTION
Printing

Reduction printing involves carving a design, printing it, and then carving a second design into the same stamp and printing on top of the first print in a different shade or color. Your final print will look complex and three-dimensional. The first print establishes the highlight and midtone, and the second print creates the shadow. If desired, you can carve and print the stamp more than twice for a more gradual shading effect.

There is no need to be intimidated by this technique. It only requires a few precise steps, and the results are extremely rewarding. Who knew that you could make a wall-ready piece of art with just one rubber stamp?

REDUCTION PRINTING

Skill level 3

Materials

Basic carving materials (see page 10)

A few sheets of printmaking paper, such as Rives BFK

Water-soluble block printing ink, white plus 3 other colors

Ink retarder and ink extender (optional)

Brayer and inking plate

Putty knife

Eraser

1 Photocopy the two templates on page 58, and carve template A by following the instructions on page 20.

2 Flip your stamp over and use a pencil to make a large "+" sign that covers the entire back of the stamp. This mark will help you with registration (aligning the stamps) when you begin printing.

3 Trim your printmaking paper into sheets measuring 8½ x 11 in/22 x 28 cm. Printmaking paper generally comes as a large sheet about 22 x 30 in/56 x 76 cm in size, so approximately six 8½-x-11-in/22-x-28-cm sheets can be cut from each large sheet. Set aside any excess scraps of paper to be used for test prints.

4 Mix the lighter of the two colors you will use. (See the "Extra Hints" box on page 58 to help you mix your first color on your inking plate.) Apply this color ink to your stamp with the brayer and print onto paper. Before lifting the stamp up off the paper, use the pencil to place dots on the paper along the edges of your stamp next to the endpoints of the "+" sign. Lift the stamp up, and repeat this step for as many prints as you desire. Make a few test prints on scrap paper for practice before printing on your larger, pre-cut sheets. You can stamp in just about any color, as many times as you like, and in any layout of your choosing: In a horizontal row, stacked on top of each other, or in a grid.

5 Once you have completely finished stamping with your first stamp (template A), allow the ink to dry. Wash your stamp and tools with warm water, and dry them before beginning the next step.

6 Trace template B and carefully line it up to your stamp and burnish the design onto it. You can now see the final design and can carve the final stamp.

7 Mix a color a few shades darker than your first prints. Apply ink to your stamp with the brayer and hold the stamp over your first print. Align the endpoints of the "+" sign to the registration dots you made with the first print, then carefully lower the stamp to the paper and print. Lift the stamp up and admire your reduction print! Repeat for all prints.

8 Erase pencil marks from your reduction print once the ink has completely dried.

Extra Hints — You Can't Start Over

For this, and any other reduction print projects, make sure you have plenty of paper trimmed and ready to print before using your first stamp. You will undoubtedly have a few misprints, and the reduction printing technique does not allow you to start over once you have altered the stamp carving for the second printing.

Project continues overleaf ⟶

Templates

Ⓐ

Ⓑ

Extra Hints

Mixing Block Printing Ink

Block printing ink comes in a variety of colors, but if you're looking for that perfect shade of coral, a rich pistachio, or a vivid sea blue, the chances are you'll have to create the color yourself. A vast array of colors can be achieved using a basic selection comprising black and white and the primary colors (red, yellow, and blue). Some darker shades such as blue or red are stronger than lighter colors including yellow and white. You will only need to add a small amount of the darker colors to produce a nice rich color. It's easier to make a color darker than it is to lighten it, so start with your lightest colors and add the darker shades to them until you obtain the color you desire.

For a more detailed description of how to mix different colors, and a chart showing how to create different shades, see "Creating Vibrant Colors" on page 24. Once you have placed your chosen ink colors, and possibly some ink retarder and/or ink extender (see page 17), on your printing plate, you can begin mixing. Start by scraping everything up with a putty knife, then smooth the ink back onto the inking plate. Continue doing this until the inks become completely mixed and smooth. You can then put the mixed ink at the top of your inking plate and proceed to roll out with your brayer, then roll it onto the stamp and begin printing.

It can be incredibly rewarding to experiment with images of different types of objects on a reduction printing stamp, and to try different color combinations. Try printing with high-contrast combinations of colors to achieve a bold, graphic effect as in the cassettes print project above.

COLORING-IN
Stamps

These hot air balloon stamps look adorable stamped onto a child's dresser or night table. Paint the open areas of the stamp in any combination of colors. The end piece will be a work of art that both you and your child will enjoy for years to come. Coloring in a hand-carved stamp is a great way to involve children in stamping. They get to pick the colors and personalize the stamped motif—and there's no need to be limited to furniture, either. Why not stamp some gift wrap and color it in with pens, or stamp a T-shirt and color it with fabric markers? Let your imagination soar!

COLORING-IN STAMPS

Skill level 2

Templates

Materials

Wood furniture, sanded, primed, and painted with a base color of your choosing

Basic carving materials (see page 10)

Block printing ink, black

Brayer and inking plate

Acrylic paint, in a selection of colors

Paper plate

Paintbrushes, assorted small sizes

Acrylic paint sealer

1 Copy the template and carve your stamps as instructed on page 20.

2 Use a brayer to roll block printing ink onto the inking plate, then roll ink evenly onto the stamp.

3 Secure the piece of furniture so it will be stable under pressure when stamping. It is best to stamp on a horizontal surface instead of trying to print the stamp vertically. Print the stamp onto your piece of furniture. Repeat inking and printing stamps until the design is complete. Set the furniture aside to dry completely.

4 Put a selection of acrylic paint colors onto a paper plate. Paint in the open areas of the stamp. Try to paint all the areas you would like of one color before switching to the next color.

5 When finished and dry, paint a coat of clear acrylic paint sealer over the entire surface to seal the print and paint to the piece.

Transforming a Child's Drawing into a Stamp

Creating an outline stamp of a child's artwork is a great idea! Create the stamp just as you would any other carved stamp—photocopy the design, transfer to rubber, then carve out any white areas. Your child can then stamp and color in their artwork many times over. It's a keepsake that they can enjoy now and cherish forever.

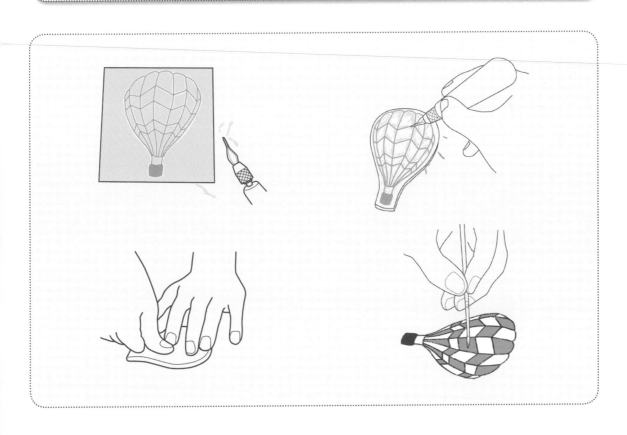

CHAPTER 2
Gifts

Need the perfect gift? How do you find that special something for that special someone? The answer is that you can make it yourself! In this chapter you'll learn a variety of stamping techniques that will allow you to make an original gift that is both personal and useful. Variations on each project can be made by just switching the colors or arrangement of the design. Making a handmade gift is just as fun as seeing the person enjoy it.

STAMPED
Bookplates

These delightful bookplates have a nice antique look that is easy to create and looks gorgeous. The process of "antiquing" the bookplates demonstrates the more subtle effects that can be achieved with ink pads, rather than simply stamping a solid line or block of color. The mounting squares that you will affix to the back of the cards have a protective paper that allows the recipient to stick them into place at his or her convenience. The bookplates could also be used as gift tags or labels for items around the house or in your scrapbook.

STAMPED BOOKPLATES

Skill level

❙

Materials

Basic carving materials (see page 10)

Blank business cards or card stock cut to 3½ x 2 in/ 9 x 5 cm

Dye-based ink pad

Adhesive mounting squares

Decorative ribbon or baker's twine (for final gift packaging)

❙ Photocopy the template and carve your stamp as instructed on page 20.

② With the cards already trimmed to size, ink the stamp and stamp the cards. Feel free to mix things up—it might be fun to stamp each card in a different pattern or color.

③ To "antique" the card edges, take a card in one hand and your ink pad in the other hand and begin to gently scrape the edge of the ink pad along the edge of the card. The angle at which you hold the ink pad will determine how much ink goes onto the card. Repeat on each edge of each card.

④ Stick four mounting squares (one per corner) to the back of each card.

⑤ To package as a gift, stack the cards up and tie them together with some ribbon or baker's twine.

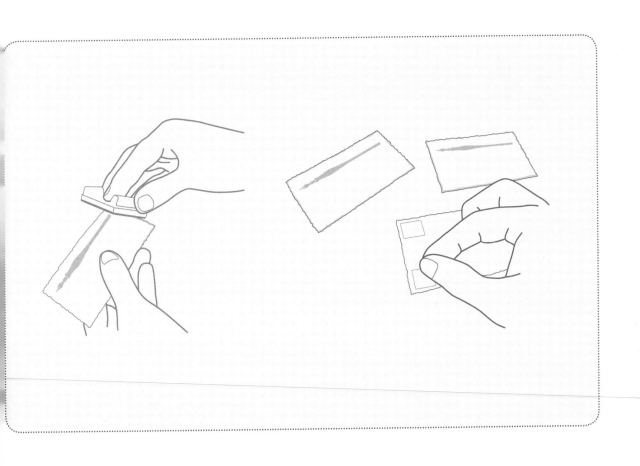

Template

EMBOSSED MONOGRAM
Stationery Set

Personalized stationery makes a thoughtful and useful gift. Use a monogram from the template provided or create your own. This project requires embossing—a fun and relatively easy way to give cards or envelopes an elegant and polished look. Similar in effect to thermographic printing and engraving, embossing is accessible and inexpensive, and requires relatively few materials. The embossing powder is heated and transforms the stamped design into a raised and shiny print.

EMBOSSED MONOGRAM STATIONERY SET

Skill level
1

1 Choose the size and number of letters for your monogram. For a monogram 1⅓ in/35 mm tall, set your copier to enlarge the template on page 75 by approximately 150 percent. For a two- or three-letter monogram, make an enlarged copy of the template and cut out the letters. With double-stick tape, mount the cut-out letters onto a new piece of paper. Make sure the letters are straight and spaced evenly apart. Create a new copy so that you have a single sheet from which to trace and transfer the design to the rubber. Carve your stamps as instructed on page 20.

2 Apply ink to your stamp with the clear embossing ink pad and print onto the card. Because timing is critical when embossing, stamp only one card at a time, and complete the following steps before repeating the process.

3 Place a piece of scrap paper underneath the stamped card, then pour the embossing powder onto the wet print. Cover the print completely and generously. You can shake it ever so lightly to ensure the powder sticks to the print.

Materials

Basic carving materials (see page 10)

Double-stick tape

Clear embossing (a.k.a. "watermark") ink pad or pigment ink pad

Cards and envelopes, a solid color other than white

Scrap paper

Embossing powder, white

Fine-point tweezers

Embossing heat gun (see page 17)

Embossing Colors

Extra Hints

In this project we used a white embossing powder. It turns opaque when embossed so the color of ink underneath will not show through. If you would like the ink color to show, you can purchase clear embossing powder and print with a colored pigment ink pad. When embossed, the clear powder will melt and the color of the ink will show through and appear shiny and raised.

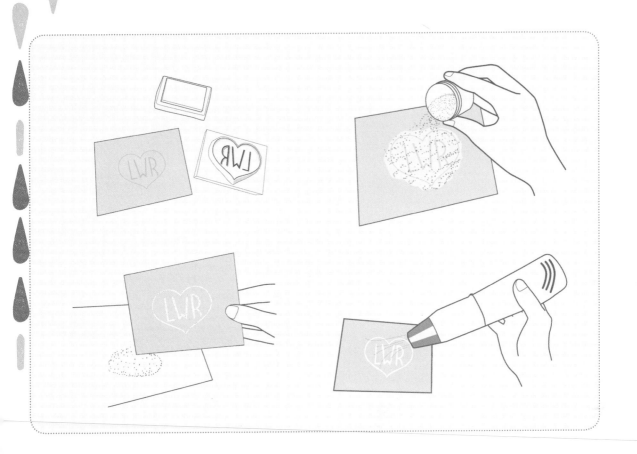

4 Gently tap the card over the scrap paper to get the excess powder off. You will see that the powder has stuck to your printed monogram. Any remaining powder can be carefully wiped away with your finger (or, for pieces stuck in isolated areas, removed with fine-point tweezers). Any powder on the card will melt and stick to your card, so you want to make sure you get all the unwanted powder off! Excess powder can be poured back into the jar of embossing powder.

5 Hold the embossing heat gun at an angle to the card, away from you and the hand that is holding the card in place. Turn the heat gun on and move the nozzle around to distribute the heat around the print. You want to have the heat gun about a finger's length from the print. The powder will take 20 to 30 seconds to melt and seal. Once you see one area of powder melt, move the heat gun to any other areas that have not yet melted. Turn off the heat gun and leave to cool once the entire print has melted. Your print is now permanently sealed to the card. Set the card aside and allow it to dry. Repeat steps 2 through 5 for each card.

Project continues overleaf ⟶

Creating Brighter Whites

I'm often asked what is the best white ink to stamp with. There are lots of white ink pads on the market, but on their own, they will not produce a stand-out white. By using a clear embossing or pigment ink pad and white embossing powder, you will get a stunning, stark-white print that stands out beautifully on dark cards. You can also use a pigment ink pad when embossing. Since white embossing powder will turn opaque, the ink color underneath does not matter much. Both a clear embossing pad and pigment ink pads have a long drying time and somewhat sticky consistency that help the embossing powder adhere. Do not use dye or chalk ink pads as they dry too quickly for the embossing powder to stick to them.

Templates

Alphabet Font: Blake

A B C D E F G H
I J K L M N O P Q
R S T U V W X Y Z

FOAM-STAMPED
Journals and Wrapped Pencils

Bookbinding is incredibly fun and can be surprisingly easy. Once you have all the materials set up, it will be a breeze to make several journals at one time. The printing foam used in this project is a simple way to create a dramatic design for the cover and pencil wraps. The binding method is called a pamphlet fold, and is similar to the way catalogues and small magazines are made.

In addition to making a stunning gift, this type of booklet would be perfect for wedding programs or a cute way to compile a child's drawings. The steps can be repeated with many different types of paper in a variety of colors and sizes.

FOAM-STAMPED JOURNALS AND WRAPPED PENCILS

Skill level
3

Materials

Printing foam sheet such as Inovart's Presto Foam

Tape

Pencil

Block printing ink, water-soluble, assorted colors

Brayer and inking plate

Card stock, assorted colors

Sketch pad (8½ x 11 in/22 x 28 cm or 9 x 12 in/23 x 30 cm)

Paper cutter or scissors

Ruler

Bone folder

Long-reach stapler

Round pencils

Foam brush

Glue

Rubber bands

1 To make the stamp, photocopy and cut out the template on page 80 and place on top of printing foam. Secure the template in place with a few pieces of tape. With a pencil, trace the template, allowing the pressure of the tip of the pencil to create an impression on the foam. Use a slightly dull pencil so that it won't tear your template when you trace it. Once you have finished tracing, cut the foam to size (about 4¼ x 5½ in/ 11 x 14 cm).

2 Put a strip of ink on the inking plate and roll it out with the brayer to an even consistency. Roll the ink onto the printing foam until it is sufficiently inked.

3 Place the inked foam inked-side-down onto one half of cardstock. Each cover requires two prints side by side to create the front and back of the journal. Before printing, establish the grain of the card stock (see page 42)—you should arrange the prints on the card stock so that the central fold between the two prints runs parallel to the grain. Gently press and rub the back of the foam with your hand to transfer the ink to the card stock. Carefully pick up the foam, re-ink it, and make another print directly next to the first.

4 For each journal and pencil set, print one piece of card stock in the opposite direction to the printed covers. This will be the piece that gets wrapped around the pencils. The reason for printing in the opposite direction is so the grain will run parallel to the pencil, making it easier to wrap and glue. Let all of the printed pieces dry for a few hours.

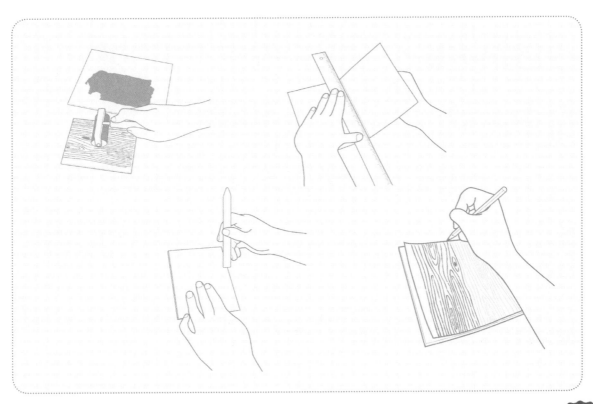

5 Establish the grain of the sketch paper (see page 42). You will want to cut the paper so that when folded, the fold, or spine, runs parallel to the grain. Trim each piece of paper to 8 x 5 in/20 x 13 cm. Each journal will have five sheets. To make five journals, cut twenty-five sheets of paper. To make ten journals, cut fifty sheets of paper.

6 Score and fold each piece of paper in half (see the "Extra Hints" box on page 81).

7 Gather five sheets of paper by placing each sheet into the fold of the next. Repeat for all sheets until you have several stacks of folded paper, five sheets each. Set aside.

8 Once the printed covers have dried, trim them down to 8¼ x 5 in/21 x 13 cm pieces using scissors or paper cutter.

9 Score and fold the covers in half.

Extra Hints

Can Your Foam Stamp Be Re-used?

Yes! As long as your foam stamp does not get scratched, you should be able to print with it many times. Over time, the impression may smooth out, but you can always retrace the design with a dull pencil or a tool such as a stylus. After printing, wash the stamp with warm water and allow it to air dry.

Project continues overleaf →

Template

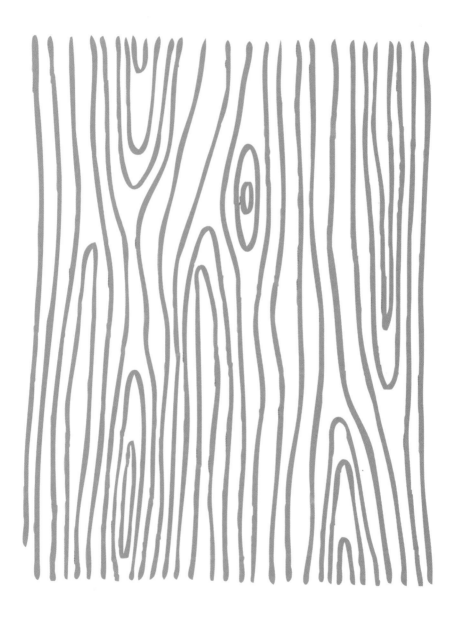

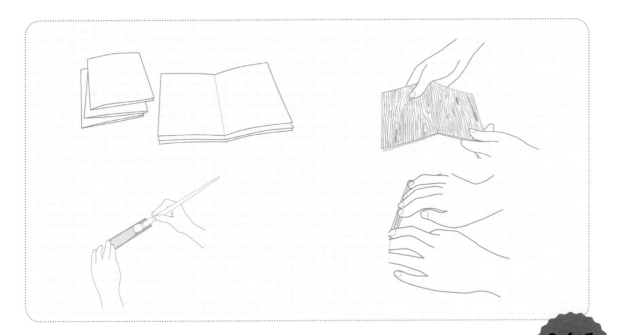

10 Place one folded five-sheet stack of papers inside a cover. Take this stack and open it flat, being sure to keep the papers aligned. With the cover facing up, so that the solid edge of the staples is on the outside of the journal, insert the stack into the long reach stapler and staple twice along the spine. Repeat for each journal.

11 Fold journal back together and reinforce the fold of the spine with your bone folder. If you would like to round the journal's corners, use a paper knife or scissors to do so; otherwise, your journal is complete.

12 For the pencils, trim the cardstock to the length of the pencils and wide enough to wrap around one pencil (about 6 x 1½ in/15 x 4 cm).

13 With the foam brush, apply glue to the inside of the paper and wrap it around a pencil. Secure with a rubber band until dry. Repeat for the remaining pencils.

14 The finished journals and pencils can be tied together or placed in a gift box.

Extra Hints

Scoring and Folding with Precision

To make a nice straight fold, put a piece of paper on a cutting mat or surface that has measurements. Place ruler on top of paper and line up to paper's halfway point (4 in/10 cm). Run the tip of your bone folder along the edge of your ruler to create an indentation in the paper. Flip your paper and reinforce the fold by running the bone folder along its back and pressing up to the edge of the ruler. Fold this scored paper in half and crease with the bone folder. Repeat for all your trimmed paper.

HAND-COLORED
Floral Cards

A card for any occasion is more special when made by hand. This project is as versatile as it is fun. It's also mess-free, and less time-consuming than it looks.

The outline style of the stamp allows you to color in each card a little differently. The colored pencil strokes easily blend together with a colorless blender pencil (which is available at any art store), giving the look of a vibrant watercolor painting. Placing darker colors toward the center of the flower can create a stunning three-dimensional effect, once blended.

HAND-COLORED FLORAL CARDS

Skill level 2

Materials

Basic carving materials (see page 10)

Dye-based ink pad, black

Blank flat cards, white, A1 size

Colored pencils (Prismacolor brand is recommended)

Colorless blending pencil (Prismacolor brand is recommended)

Blank folded cards and envelopes, assorted colors, A2 size

Double-stick tape or mounting squares

1 Photocopy the template and carve your stamp as instructed on page 20.

2 As this is a larger stamp, it will be easier and more accurate to apply the ink to the stamp by setting it down, carved-side up, and dabbing ink onto it using the stamp pad as the dauber. Once inked, print onto the smaller flat white card. Re-ink and repeat for remaining cards.

3 Lightly color in your stamp print with your lightest selection of colored pencils (for example, yellow-orange for the petals, light green for the leaf, and light blue for the jar).

4 Color your stamp print with slightly darker pencils, concentrating on adding this second color where you want to create a feeling of dimension (for example, toward the center of the flower, or the edge of the jar). Then repeat this step with the darkest colors you have chosen.

5 Run the colorless blender pencil over your colored pencil strokes. Concentrate on one section or group of colors at a time, such as the flower or the vase: Coloring over the entire print at once may bleed the colors of different sections together. If a color seems to have stained the tip of the blender, simply rub it on a blank piece of scrap paper to remove the color.

6 Mount your stamped and colored note card to the front of a larger folded card with double-stick tape or mounting squares. The colored background on the larger card will make the soft colors of the pencil strokes stand out nicely.

Extra Hints

Choosing a Color Scheme

Before you start to color in the stamp print, carefully consider which colors will complement each other well. When using the blending method described in the steps, it's best to choose colors that are similar but that contrast slightly with each other. In artistic terms, a group of colors that are next to each other on the color wheel are called "analogous colors." Yellow-orange, orange, and red-orange would be considered analogous colors in relation to each other. Selecting a group of perhaps three analogous colors will give your card a vibrant and unified look. Begin coloring your card with the lightest color, and then add increasingly dark colors for a look of added dimension.

Template

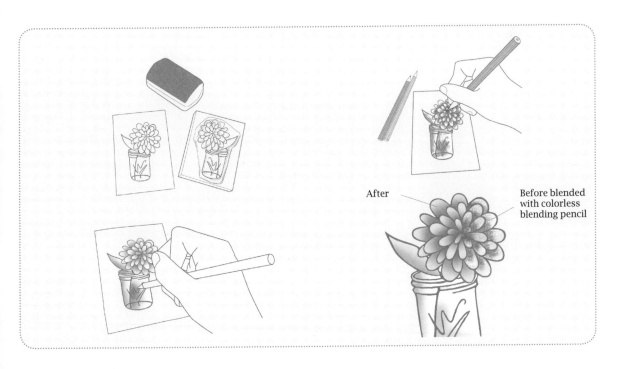

After

Before blended with colorless blending pencil

TWO-COLORED
Stamped Pillowcases

Embellished pillowcases make lovely gifts—whether you're giving them to a couple who has recently moved into a new home or to a teen who is about to begin college. A set of hand-printed pillowcases is a gift that can be cherished for years to come. Both personal and practical, what could be better?

The inspiration for this project was a daffodil, so I chose to print in two shades of yellow, but the flowers could be printed in any color to match the recipient's taste.

Choose a pillowcase with a thread count of 200 or higher, which will give you a nice smooth surface on which to print.

TWO-COLORED STAMPED PILLOWCASES

Materials

Pillowcases

Basic carving materials (see page 10)

Fabric paints, two colors

Paper plates

Sponge daubers

Buttons, assorted (optional)

Embroidery thread and needle (optional)

1 Wash, dry, and iron the pillowcases so that you have a clean, preshrunk, and smooth surface on which to print.

2 Photocopy the template, to a smaller or larger scale if you prefer, and carve your stamp as instructed on page 20. Although you will use the stamp in two pieces, they are carved as a single stamp from one piece of rubber.

3 Once you have carved the design, take the craft knife and cut the inner stamp out of the center. You may have to clean up the edges with the linoleum cutters so that there are no jagged edges to either stamp.

4 Place the two pieces back together and flip over. With a pencil draw a "V" that covers the back of both stamps. This mark will help you line up the stamps when printed together. Take the inner stamp out and set both stamps aside.

5 Pour out a small amount of each color of fabric paint onto paper plates. Take a sponge dauber and apply one color of the paint to one part of the stamp. Repeat with the other color and the other part of the stamp.

6 Without smudging the paint you have just applied, carefully place the larger stamp onto your pillowcase. Do not pick the stamp up yet! Next pick up the smaller stamp and position into the center of the larger stamp, making sure to line the stamps up with the "V" mark you have made. Once stamps are in place, gently apply pressure with your hands to get the design to print and then carefully pick them up.

7 Repeat steps 5 and 6 for as many flowers as you would like to print. You can alternate the colors, but be sure to thoroughly wash and dry the stamp before re-inking with a different color.

Extra Hints

Care of Printed Fabric

Check the manufacturer's instructions on the fabric paint you have selected so that you know how to care for the printed fabric. Some fabric paints require heat-setting before use, while others may need just a few hours' drying time before use.

8 If desired, you can embellish the design further by sewing buttons onto the center of each flower using embroidery thread. Make sure the prints have completely dried (for at least a couple of hours) before adding any embellishments.

Template

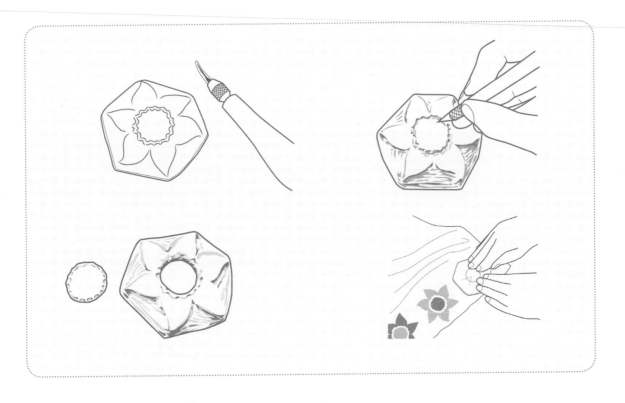

CHAPTER 3
Accessories

Stamping isn't just limited to paper crafts; you can stamp on fabric and accessories too! What better way to show off your personal style than with a bold stamped scarf or a quirky and vibrant tote bag? After exploring the techniques in this chapter, you will have the know-how to adorn a variety of apparel and accessories. Tailor each project to suit your taste—stamping is for every age and style.

BUBBLE-WRAP
Tote Bag

A stamp can be made from just about anything. In this project you will use bubble wrap, which has a fun but uniform geometric pattern. The term for printing with miscellaneous items is "found object printing" and, as the name suggests, this method includes using just about anything you can find to apply ink to and print with. Using this project as inspiration, try some more found object printing with materials from around your house, neighborhood, or local park or beach. This project is ideal for getting kids involved—they can help you find objects to print with. It's a great way to recycle, and an excellent excuse for a scavenger hunt!

BUBBLE-WRAP TOTE BAG

Skill level 2

Materials

Bubble wrap (bubbles 5/16 in/ 1 cm high)

Scissors

Paintbrush

Glue

Acrylic sheet, approximately 5 x 7 in/13 x 18 cm

Plain canvas tote bag

Sturdy cardboard to fit inside the tote bag

Fabric paint

Paper plate

Foam roller

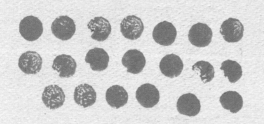

1 Cut a piece of bubble wrap with scissors to fit the length of your acrylic sheet. The ends of the bubble wrap should be cut in a zigzag pattern. This will allow you to stamp two prints next to each other without a noticeable seam. The height of your bubble wrap can be trimmed to your preference—three or four rows are ideal.

2 Turn the bubble wrap over and brush glue over the entire backside. Stick it to the acrylic sheet and allow it to dry completely. Be extra gentle so that you don't pop any of the bubbles.

3 Lay the tote bag on a flat surface. To keep the fabric smooth and taut (which will help you get a nice print), insert the piece of cardboard into the bag to help you stretch the fabric flat.

4 Put fabric paint on the paper plate and roll it out with the foam roller. Apply paint to the bubble wrap by gently rolling over the bubbles. The trick is to start with a little paint and add more as needed. Make a test print on scrap paper or fabric to check that you have the right amount of paint. Reapply paint before each print.

5 Pick up the inked bubble wrap stamp and print onto the tote bag. Apply a light, even pressure to the stamp—enough pressure to stamp the paint, but not so much pressure that you pop the bubble wrap. Repeat applying paint and printing until the front of your tote bag is stamped to your liking. If you decide you would like to print the back of the tote bag, let the front dry before repeating this step.

6 To care for the print on the bag, follow the instructions included with the fabric paint.

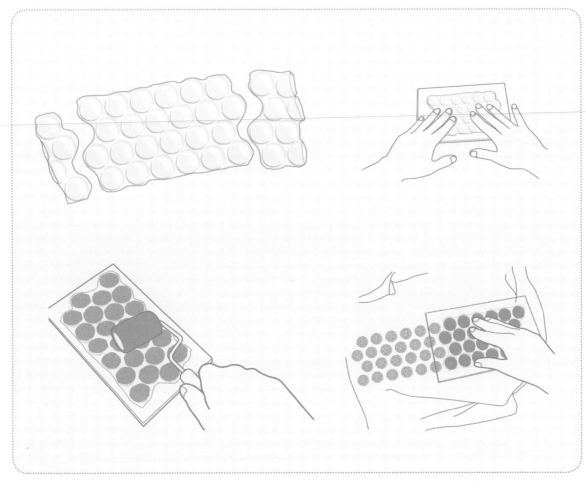

KITCHEN
Apron

What better way to show off both your culinary and creative skills than by wearing this fun, hand-stamped apron? Printing with a large stamp, similar to the one used in this project, may seem intimidating, but big stamps can actually be quite simple to work with. The large open sections of the design can be quick and easy to carve.

This project may inspire you to make other oversized stamps. You are limited only by the size of carving rubber sheet that you can find! Create a poster or a T-shirt. The end result will look like a bold screen print, but you will only need about half the materials.

KITCHEN APRON

Skill level 2

Materials

Cotton apron

Basic carving materials (see page 10)

Fabric paint or water-based textile screen-printing ink

Paper plate

Foam roller

Scrap paper

1 Wash, dry, and iron your apron so you have a smooth surface on which to print.

2 Copy the template on page 101, and carve your stamp as instructed on page 20.

3 Roll out the fabric paint onto the paper plate with the foam roller. Roll a small amount of paint onto the stamp and add more as needed until the stamp is sufficiently inked.

4 Print your stamp onto the apron. Gently press down with even pressure and then lift up. Repeat steps 3 and 4 for as many prints as required.

5 To print an isolated part of the fabric, such as the pockets, cut a corner out of a piece of paper and position it against the edge of the pocket. Leave the pocket exposed but cover the surrounding area with the paper. Ink the stamp and print it onto the pocket. Any overlapping part of the stamp will print onto the paper, leaving the fabric around the pocket's edge clean. Adjust the paper around the edges of the pocket as you continue printing on pockets as shown in the illustration.

6 To print the straps, lay each strap out flat and place a piece of scrap paper underneath. Apply paint to stamp and print onto apron strap. Be sure to reapply paint before each print.

7 Follow the manufacturer's instructions for the fabric paint to complete and care for your apron.

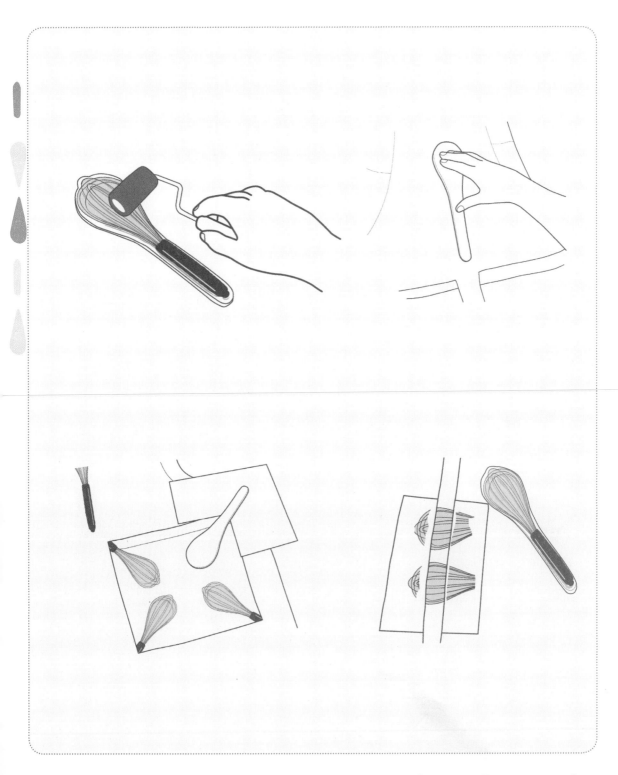

Project continues overleaf →

Template

PRINTED
Plaid Scarf

This printed scarf is a versatile accessory that can be used as a necktie, a headband, or tied onto a bag for extra color. For this project, you'll use strips of foam to print a classic plaid design. I'm sure it will quickly become a favorite piece in your wardrobe.

The craft foam used in this project is available with or without an adhesive side and can be purchased at just about any arts and craft store, usually in the kids' crafts section. Sold in sheets, and in a variety of colors, the foam has a smooth surface that allows you to create a crisp, solid print. Since it is used here only to apply ink to the fabric, the color of the foam is unimportant.

PRINTED PLAID SCARF

Skill level
1

Materials

Bandana, solid color, approximately 21 x 21 in/ 53 x 53 cm

Adhesive-backed craft foam, 1 sheet

Ruler

Scissors

Acrylic sheet, 5 x 7 in/ 13 x 18 cm

Foam roller or sponge dauber

Fabric paint (multiple colors)

Paper plate

Cotton swab or paper towel

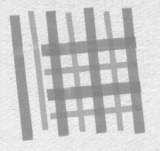

1 Wash, dry, and iron your bandana so you have a smooth surface on which to print.

2 Cut foam into strips: 1 x 7 in/2.5 x 18 cm and ½ x 7 in/12 mm x 18 cm. The 7 in/18 cm length matches the length of the acrylic sheet. Adjust your foam strips accordingly if you are using a different size acrylic sheet.

3 Peel off the protective sheet from the back of the foam to expose the adhesive, and stick the foam strips to the acrylic sheet.

4 Roll out the fabric paint onto the paper plate with the foam roller. Roll or sponge a small amount of paint onto the foam strips and add more as needed until the stamp is sufficiently inked. If paint gets onto the acrylic sheet, simply wipe it off with a cotton swab or paper towel. You don't want excess ink to print unwanted marks on your bandana.

5 Print the inked stamp onto your bandana. Repeat, applying more ink as required, and printing so that the strips line up with each other. Let dry, then apply perpendicular strips, printing in different colors, to create a plaid design.

PENCIL-PRINTED
Bow Tie Hair Clip

This charming bow tie makes a sweet hair accessory. The pattern is up to you— print a lot of dots or just a few. Making the "stamp" is quick and easy, and the bow is made with little more than scissors and glue— no sewing machine required! The bow could also be re-purposed as a man's accessory by substituting the hair clip for a tie clip. Consider this technique for other fabric crafts—the dot pattern would be lovely stamped on a pair of curtains or a lampshade.

Almost any smooth cotton fabric will work for this project, and you don't need much. Check out your local fabric store's section of scrap fabric for some great small pieces to work with.

PENCIL-PRINTED BOW TIE HAIR CLIP

Skill level
1

Materials

Craft knife

Pencil with a new eraser

Fabric paint

Paper plate

Sponge dauber

Fabric, solid color, at least
6 x 10 in/15 x 25.5 cm

Fabric scissors

Hot glue

Hair clip

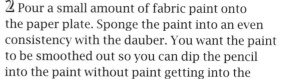

1 With the flat edge of the craft knife (not the point), carefully slice a groove about halfway into the eraser. Make about three grooves into the eraser on the pencil for a striped design.

2 Pour a small amount of fabric paint onto the paper plate. Sponge the paint into an even consistency with the dauber. You want the paint to be smoothed out so you can dip the pencil into the paint without paint getting into the grooves cut into the eraser and then bleeding onto the fabric.

3 When you have an even consistency of paint, dab the eraser into the paint and then onto the fabric. Be random with the printing and have fun. Be sure to re-ink the eraser before each print. Let the fabric dry completely before moving onto the next step.

4 Trim fabric into two pieces: 8 x 6 in/20 x 15 cm, and 1½ x 6 in/4 x 15 cm.

5 Fold the smaller fabric piece into thirds lengthwise and secure with two small dots of glue. It's okay if it does not lay completely flat.

6 Flip the larger piece of fabric over so the unprinted side is face up. Fold the long ends into the center, then the short ends into the center.

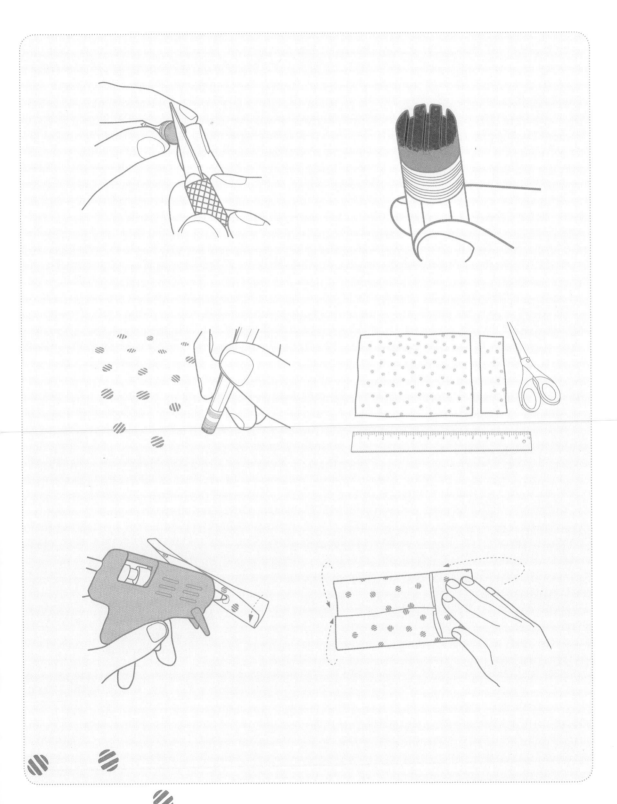

Project continues overleaf ⟶

7 With your fingers positioned at the top and bottom of the folds, scrunch the fabric together and pick it up, holding the folds in place. You can now see the bow coming together.

8 Take the long folded strip and wrap it around the center of the bow tie. The piece will be much longer than you need. Wrap one side of the strip inward toward the center of the bow.

9 Slide hair clip onto the other extended side of the strip and glue it into place so that the clip is fastened to the center back of the bow.

10 Finish the bow by trimming the strip down to about ½ in/12.5 mm from the center, then folding it under and gluing it into place. You want to make sure that the strip covers the hair clip and is hidden from the front view of the bow. Once the hot glue dries, your bow is ready to be worn!

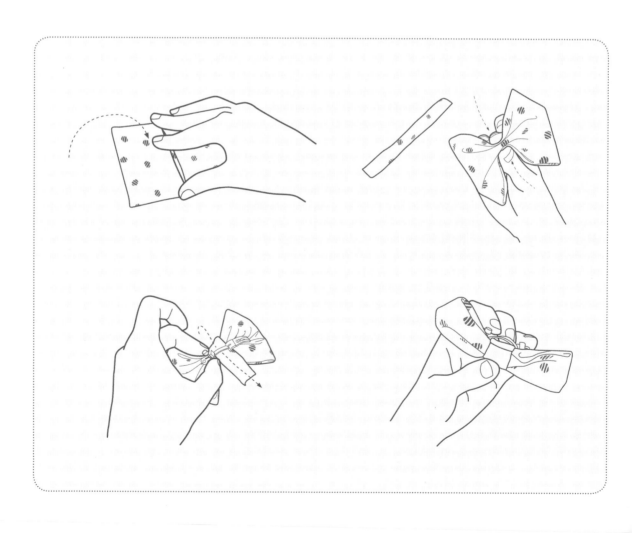

This printing technique works well on any fine, smooth fabric—for instance, it can brighten up a plain lampshade, as in this example.

Extra Hints

CHAPTER 4
Organizers

Stamping is an ideal method for decorating a wide range of items, from stationery to furniture. A stamp not only gives things a personal, handmade look that at the same time looks thoroughly professional, but it also allows you to build patterns and motifs that are visually striking and entirely unique. By using combinations of stamps creatively you can create an appropriate design for almost any occasion—from a classic and sophisticated wedding invitation to a fun and colorful picture frame. Experiment to find the most effective color scheme for your project, stamp it, then stand back and admire the results!

RETRO-MODERN
Storage Labels

These labels will prove to be handy in just about any room in the house. They can label items in the kitchen such as food jars and containers, or they could be used in a craft room to organize your supplies. Make them especially useful by implementing a color-coding system. These lovely printed stickers also make perfect gift tags and address labels.

The stamp template can also be used very effectively on business-card-sized projects, so get creative and make some standout calling cards from thick cardstock, or enliven some place cards at your next get-together.

RETRO-MODERN STORAGE LABELS

Skill level
1

Materials

**Basic carving materials
(see page 10)**

**Wood or acrylic block
(for mounting stamp)**

**Assorted dye-based or
chalk ink pads**

**Blank adhesive labels,
3½ x 2 in/9 x 5 cm**

Stamp cleaner

1 Copy the template and carve your stamp as
instructed on page 20.

2 Mount your stamp to a wood or acrylic block
as instructed on page 26. The large carved-out
area on the stamp creates a thin area on the
stamp that makes it difficult to print with unless
it's mounted on a backing.

3 Apply ink to the stamp and begin to print the
labels by carefully lowering the stamp onto each
one. Re-ink the stamp before each print.

4 Let the labels dry before using.

5 Since your stamp is mounted, do not clean it
with water. Instead, clean the stamp by printing
off ink onto scrap paper and then removing any
remaining ink with stamp cleaner.

Extra Hints

Handy Label Storage

Labels can be kept together on the
sheet, or you can cut them up into
individual labels. Store them in clear
zip-top bags and keep them in drawers
around the house so they are easily
accessible when you need them.

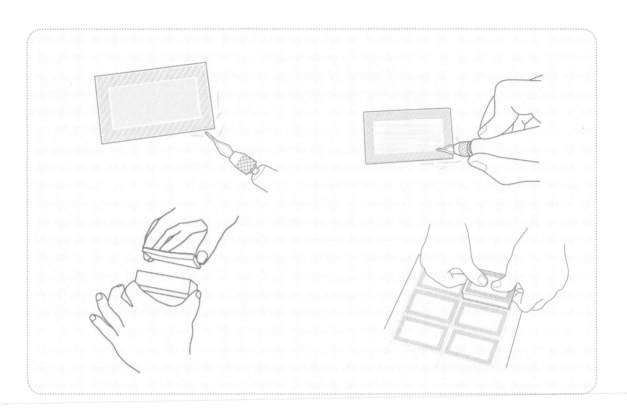

Template

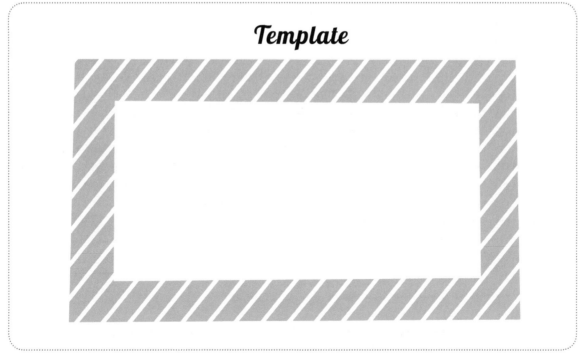

THUMBTACKS AND
Magnets

Make organizing papers on your bulletin board or fridge more stylish with these easy-to-make tacks and magnets. Choose three paint colors to match your décor. Creating the floral design is as easy as dipping the end of a paintbrush into paint and dabbing it onto wood disks. Here we attach thumbtacks and adhesive magnets to the stamped wood disks, but you could also glue on earring posts or a brooch pin for a stylish accessory.

THUMBTACKS AND MAGNETS

Skill level
1

Materials

Acrylic paint, 3 colors

Paint palette or paper plate

Unfinished wood disks
in assorted sizes

Paintbrush

Clear varnish

Flat tacks

Strong glue or epoxy

Adhesive magnets

1 Pour a small amount of each color of paint onto the paint palette or paper plate. Apply two coats of paint on one side of each wood disk, a few in each color. Allow the disks to dry completely and clean the paintbrush.

2 If needed, pour some more paint onto the paint palette. Take the end of your paintbrush handle (the opposite end from the brush) and lightly dip it into one color of paint.

3 Dab the tip of the handle onto a wood disk as shown in the illustration. Start with the center dot and continue to print the surrounding dots (petals) in a contrasting color. Repeat dipping the handle into the paint for each dot that you apply. You will need to wash and dry the paintbrush end every time you change paint colors. When finished, let the painted wood disks dry completely.

4 Apply a coat of acrylic clear varnish to the surface of the wood disks to seal the paint and give them a durable shiny finish.

5 Glue the tacks onto the backs of the wood disks with a strong glue or epoxy. If you select magnets with an adhesive backing, simply peel off the protective paper to expose the adhesive and stick the magnets to the backs of your wood disks.

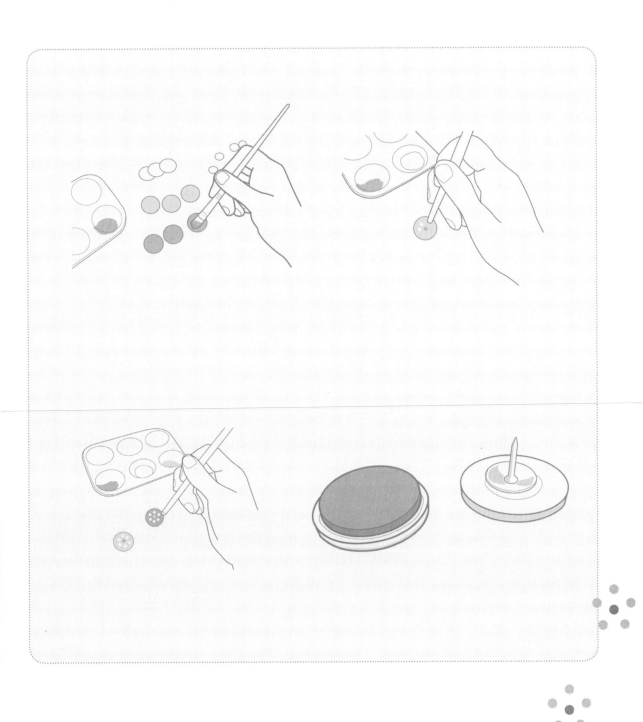

SCRAP RUBBER-DECORATED Storage Boxes

This project is a clever way to put to good use all those rubber scraps left over from past stamp-carving projects. The idea came to me one day when my scrap pile of carving rubber began to overflow. The fun part is experimenting and finding the perfect placement for the scrap pieces—it's like a rubber stamp puzzle. Make sure all of your scrap pieces are made from the same type of carving rubber, or you may not get a consistent print. Try stamping coordinating pieces, such as divider cards and folders, or gift wrap and cards.

SCRAP RUBBER-DECORATED STORAGE BOXES

Skill level 2

Materials

Scrap pieces of carving rubber

Wood or acrylic block, approximately 3 x 3 in/ 8 x 8 cm

Double-stick tape

Cardboard photo storage box (single color or plain)

Stack of books (for weight only; will not be damaged)

Block printing ink

Brayer and inking plate

Hair dryer (optional)

1 Lay out several pieces of scrap rubber and move them around to see which pieces fit into each other or line up nicely. Place the pieces on the mounting block and move them around until you are happy with the design. Feel free to trim some pieces to fit the stamp as needed.

2 Adhere each piece to the mounting block with double-stick tape.

3 To make the storage box sturdy and easy to print on without it caving in, fill the box with a stack of books. The books will help keep the box in place and allow you to apply firm pressure in order to obtain a nice solid print on the box.

4 Roll block printing ink out on the inking plate with the brayer and roll ink onto the stamp. Print your stamp onto the box and lid. Apply firm, even pressure without letting the stamp slide.

5 After you have printed one side of the box, allow it to dry before switching to the next side. You can speed up drying time using a hair dryer. The ink is dry when it turns from slightly shiny to dull and is dry to the touch.

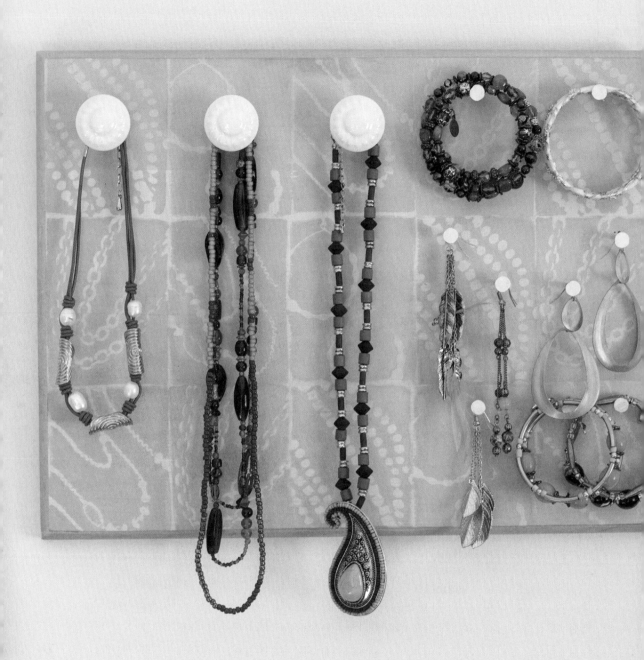

JEWELRY
Organizer

This jewelry organizer is a beautiful way to organize and display your favorite necklaces, earrings, and bracelets. The Moldable Foam Stamps by Magic Stamps used in this project are really fun and easy to work with. Quickly heating up the foam creates an impressionable surface that you can press onto just about any object. A recessed design will form on the stamp that creates a stunning negative pattern when printed. You can use both sides of the foam, and if you don't like the design you've created, heat it back up to smooth out the design and start again!

JEWELRY ORGANIZER

Materials

Assorted objects to press into foam, such as earrings

Magic Stamp Moldable Foam Stamps (from craft stores)

Embossing heat gun or hair dryer

Block printing ink

Brayer and inking plate

Scrap paper

Unfinished wood plaque, 11 x 14 in/28 x 36 cm

Paper towel

Epoxy or strong glue

Assorted drawer knobs

Roof nails, 1 in/2.5 cm long

Hammer

Paint (metallic or other finish)

Paintbrush

Saw tooth hangers

1 On a flat surface, arrange a few objects to press into the foam, such as a chain necklace, beaded bracelet, or dangly earrings. Adjust each piece until it is in a position, or pattern, you like.

2 Put a Magic Stamp Moldable Foam Stamp down in front of you and apply heat with a heat gun, being sure not to place your hand in front of the heat. Move the heat gun around to evenly heat the block. It should take about 20 to 30 seconds to sufficiently heat the block. If you're using a hair dryer, it will take a little longer. Test the foam to see what amount of heat works well.

3 As soon as you have heated the foam block, quickly pick it up and press it down onto your already arranged object of choice. Apply firm even pressure to get the object to leave a nice deep impression in the block. Lift the block up and remove the object if it has stuck to the block.

4 Squeeze block printing ink onto an inking plate and roll out with the brayer. Roll the inked brayer onto the surface of the foam. Add enough ink to get an even layer of ink on the stamp but not so much that it fills the recessed areas of the stamp. Make test prints on scrap paper until you find the right amount of ink.

5 Once your stamp is sufficiently inked, print it onto the wood plaque. Apply even pressure without letting the stamp slide. Reapply ink before each print.

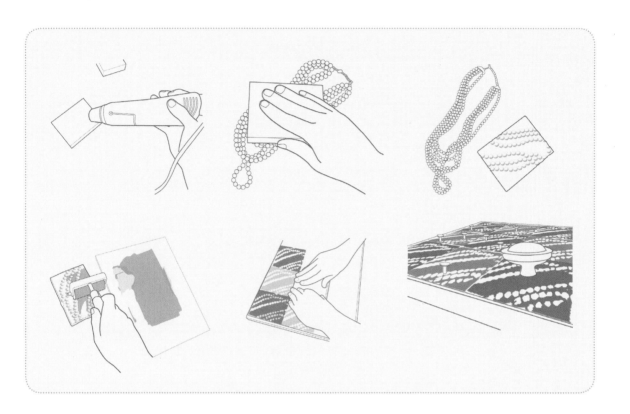

6 Repeat steps 1 to 5, using different objects to create multiple foam block stamp designs on your board. You can create a pattern using blocks with different impressions, or by using different colors of ink. Because the foam blocks are reusable (after reheating and smoothing out the design), you can try many variations.

7 When you have finished printing, clean off the tools and the foam block(s) with warm water and pat dry with a paper towel.

8 Once the wood plaque is completely dry, use epoxy or a strong glue to adhere drawer knobs (using a drill and screw are not necessary since the knobs will only hold very light items) and hammer in a few nails to hang necklaces, earrings, and bracelets.

9 To complete the look, paint the trim of your jewelry display board in a bright color or with metallic paint.

10 When all surfaces are completely dry, attach saw tooth hangers to the back. Now it's ready to be hung up and enjoyed!

DRAGONFLY
Shelf Liner

Shelf liners are a simple way to freshen up your cabinets and drawers. The string technique for making stamps is easy and fun because the slow drying time of the glue allows you ample time to position the string into place. And the design doesn't have to be perfect—a little variation only adds to its handcrafted appeal. Try using your own design or doodle as the basis for the stamp design; a free-form or abstract design could make an equally impressive pattern. Some types of contact paper are safe for walls too—individual dragonfly designs on contact paper could make fun decals for a bedroom wall.

DRAGONFLY SHELF LINER

Materials

Graphite transfer paper

Wood block, approximately
4 x 5 in/10 x 13 cm

Ballpoint or other
hard-tipped pen

Craft glue

Paper plate

Thick string or twine

Hair dryer (optional)

Solid shelf liner or contact
paper

Felt or stack of papers

Block printing ink

Brayer and inking plate

Skill level 2

1 Make a copy of the template on page 135 and cut it out.

2 Lay the graphite paper on top of the wood block. You want the dark side of the graphite paper face-down on the wood and the lighter side facing up. Lay the printed design on top of that, design facing up.

3 Holding the papers in place on the wood, trace the design with a pen. The pressure from your pen will make the graphite transfer onto the wood. When finished tracing, lift up the papers and set aside. You should now be able to see your design and where you will glue the string.

4 Pour a small amount of glue onto a paper plate. Coat about a finger's length of your string or twine with the glue. Starting in the center of one of the spiral areas, such as the wing, glue the string into place along the lines made from the graphite paper. It may help to glue the string in sections, allowing it to partially dry along the way, adding more glue as necessary. (A hair

dryer can speed up the process.) Continue to glue string into place on the design until the entire design is complete with string. Let the stamp dry completely.

5 Unroll a few feet of shelf liner or contact paper. To help the stamp create a solid print, place a piece of flat felt or a stack of papers underneath the shelf liner paper. Because the glued string is hard, it will not print like a typical rubber stamp that is flexible. Adding the felt under the shelf

Project continues overleaf ⟶

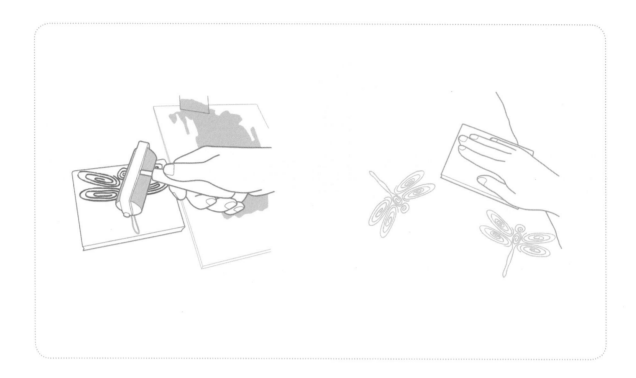

liner paper will act as a shock absorber and allow the stamp to print more thoroughly.

6 Roll block printing ink onto an inking plate with a brayer, and then roll ink evenly onto the stamp. Wipe off any excess ink from your stamp with your finger or a cotton swab.

7 Stamp the image in a regular or random pattern on the shelf liner paper. Re-ink the stamp before each print.

8 When the design is complete, allow the stamped paper to dry for a few hours before placing onto shelves, into drawers, or onto your walls. Clean all the tools with warm water (but not the stamp—stamp the excess ink off onto a piece of damp paper towel) and leave them all to dry.

Template

TROUBLESHOOTING

Smudged ink and misprints are part of the adventures of printmaking. The following tips offer help and time-saving ideas to ensure a great finish to your projects.

Print Is Blurry or Smudged

You may be applying too much ink/paint to the stamp. If too much ink has already gotten into the recessed areas of the stamp, it's best to clean off the stamp as recommended in the steps, and start over. Reapply ink to the stamp by starting with a little bit and adding more as necessary. Keep some scrap paper or newsprint on hand to make test prints and find the right amount of ink/paint for your project.

Print Is Light or Patchy

There may not be enough ink on the stamp. Try adding a bit more ink/paint to the stamp. If you find that the stamp still will not produce a solid print, it could be because the stamp is not pressing down completely onto the paper. To fix this, you can put a piece of felt or a few sheets of paper under the paper you are printing on. The felt or papers will act as a shock absorber and let the stamp press into the paper more completely. If you still cannot get a nice print, it may be time to replace your ink/paint because it could be old and dried out.

Print Is Smudged or Doubled

The stamp may have moved when it was printed. Try to apply firm, even pressure to the stamp when printing without rocking the stamp back and forth. If your stamp is unmounted, consider attaching a backing. This will help you hold the stamp firmly and apply an even pressure when you are printing.

Registration/Alignment Problems

If you need to print two colors or designs on top of each other, registration can be a challenge. Fortunately there are many tricks to help make things go smoothly.

◦ In designs where registration is important, opt not to mount your stamp. However, if you do, mount it to a clear backing such as an acrylic sheet. The extra visibility will help you line up the prints more easily.

◦ Practice makes perfect! Keep lots of scrap paper handy for test prints until you are able to comfortably print where you need to.

◦ Create a mark on the back of your stamp such as a "+" mark. When you place your stamp on your paper, make small dots with a pencil at the endpoints of the "+" mark. The dots will help you line up the stamp on the next print and can be erased when you're finished printing.

Unintended Areas of the Stamp Print

It's likely that your first few stamps will not be perfect, and why would you want that anyway? You're making a one-of-a-kind stamp! As you carve more stamps, you'll get the feel for how deep to carve down into the stamp to create a recessed area that will not print. Some people find that they like to leave a few background lines on the stamp to print. These lines, "grain lines" as I like to call them, can be a stylistic choice and will add character to your print. A few of these lines are okay to leave, but you don't want so many that they detract from the overall design of your stamp. To eliminate all grain lines, carve the nonprinting areas of the stamp down evenly and deep enough that they will not get inked and print on your paper. I also recommend slightly carving down the sides of the stamp (almost like a beveled edge) to ensure the edges don't print. If ink continues to get on the stamp in unintended areas, simply wipe it off with your finger or a cotton swab before printing.

Carved Unintended Area of Stamp

This is more of a stamp problem than it is a printing problem, but it can be very frustrating nonetheless. If you happen to accidentally slice into your design when carving your stamp, there are some possible ways to fix it. If it was a small nick in the design, just carve a little more from the design so that the area is smooth. Chances are, no one will notice the alteration. If an area got completely carved away, try to figure a way to incorporate that into your design. Maybe that flower only needs five petals instead of six. If the piece carved away was really important to the design, consider making a second stamp that can be printed separately or mounted together with the original stamp to fill the missing section.

Ink in the Middle of Your Art

If a little smudge of ink has gotten in the way of a print, try any of the following:

○ **Erase the mark with a clean, quality eraser (plastic or kneaded).** There are some erasers that can erase ink if it's not too large a smudge. This kind of eraser has a slightly grainy texture that helps lift the ink off the paper. I do not recommend pink erasers because they can leave a pink mark on your paper after you have used them.

○ **Scratch the ink off with a craft knife.** This technique may seem a little unusual but, if you're careful, it can work well and be a time saver if it means you don't have to reprint the piece! Let the print dry and then gently scratch the ink off with a craft knife. You want to lightly scrape the ink from the surface without damaging it.

○ **Get creative!** It may be possible to paint over the smudge. Or maybe you can cut the design out and mount it to another piece of paper. Another option may be to mat your design to cover up any splatters that may have happened on the outer edge of the paper. No one will ever know and your piece may even look better for it!

○ **Leave it.** A little splatter of ink can be a happy accident. And it wouldn't be the first time a little dribble made it onto a piece of art. Enjoy the experience and keep on printing!

STAMPING TIPS

Extra, Extra!

As stamping will require making a few test prints to get the right amount of ink, it's always a good idea to have a few extra pieces of paper to print on before starting your project. If you have to trim your paper to a certain size, trim it all before you begin your project so it's ready when you are. Some of the prints may end up as test prints, but some will surely turn out great! And if you end up with extras, you'll have some lovely pieces of art ready to turn into cards or gift tags.

Create Your Space

Just as you wouldn't begin cooking a recipe without first acquiring all the ingredients, you won't want to begin a project without all the materials and tools you need. Set your printing area up and make sure you have enough room to print as well as a place to store your stamped project while it dries, if necessary.

Keep It Clean

When stamping, ink can end up in the darndest places. I like to keep an old towel on hand when I print, to wipe my fingers off with if I get a little ink on them. Before printing, clean off your stamp and printing surface so that you're sure everything is free of ink, graphite, dust, etc. The smallest little smudge of anything can really mess things up!

Go for the Good Stuff

A great final product starts with great quality materials. When possible, seek out nice printing paper and quality inks and tools. Splurging on nice materials may actually save you time and money down the road if you don't have to replace them as often as other cheaper, lesser-quality products.

RESOURCES

Basic Materials

Dick Blick
www.dickblick.com
A great art store packed with a variety of carving materials, tools, ink, paint, and fine paper. This is the perfect place to start gathering your supplies.

Michaels
www.michaels.com
A general-purpose arts and craft store that carries a great selection of paint, ink pads, card stock, and embellishments. Check out their wood and hobby section for unfinished wood pieces such as picture frames and wood plaques.

Jo-Ann
www.joann.com
This fabric and craft store has a nice selection of fabrics, fabric paint, and craft materials and accessories to help complete many of your projects. They also carry an array of items such as blank bandanas, hair clasps, ribbon, and buttons.

Paper Source
www.paper-source.com
A specialty store that carries a beautiful selection of fine paper as well as an impressive line of blank stationery that comes in a wide range of luscious colors. Stock up at this store on paper, blank labels, ink pads, and embossing supplies.

Create for Less
www.createforless.com
Specialty items such as Moldable Foam Blocks by Magic Stamp and many other scrapbooking and crafting items are available at this online store.

Rubber Stamp Accessories

JMP Rubber Stamp Materials
www.rubberstampmaterials.com
An online store for the serious stamp maker! Here you will find wood mounts, printable indexing sheets, and adhesive mounting foam. They also have industrial stamp-making machines and a die-making service.

WoodPressions
www.woodpressions.com
A great source for wood mounts. You can request specific sizes and shapes in any quantity. Their quality and customer service are exceptional.

Miscellaneous

Etsy
www.etsy.com
An online marketplace where people sell hand-made items as well as unique craft supplies and vintage finds. You can support small businesses and find the perfect materials for your project.

American Apparel
www.americanapparel.net
This retailer produces USA-made, sweatshop-free blank apparel and accessory items in a wide range of colors. They have a stylish selection of T-shirts, scarves, and tote bags.

Bambeco
www.bambeco.com
This online store offers a nice selection of eco-friendly and organic products ranging from aprons and towels to linens and stationery.

INDEX

ACKNOWLEDGMENTS

Writing a book has been a long-time dream of mine. I feel so grateful to have been given the chance to make this dream come true. I want to thank the people who helped me get here. I could have not made this happen without the encouragement and support from all of you.

To my sister and craft buddy, Amy. Thank you for always encouraging me to create art and dream big. You have inspired me to pursue my passion. You have strengthened my motivation with your support and those three concise words: "Do it, Meg!"

To my husband, Jeff, thank you for your endless support and shoulder to lean on. Thank you for always making time to listen to my ideas. And thank you for tolerating all my little art messes around the house. Your encouragement has made my creativity blossom.

To my parents, thank you for all your wisdom and guidance. I'm so grateful for all of the ways you helped me achieve my goals. You challenge me to ask the hard questions in life and believe in myself.

To all of the incredible teachers I've had in my life including Susan Makov and Ed Seubert. You have so generously shared your knowledge and passion for your craft. You have given me inspiration and an undying curiosity to learn and always ask, "What if?" Thank you for encouraging me to take risks and make mistakes—a lesson that has been valuable even out of the classroom.

Special thanks to 8-year-old Sonoma for providing her wonderful drawing of a girl for the child's artwork stamp (page 63).

And finally, I'd like to thank all of the people who have purchased one of my stamps. You have given me the privilege to turn my passion into a business. Sincerely, thank you.